Humphry Repton at Herriard Park

'Improving the Premises'

AUTHORS' ACKNOWLEDGEMENTS

The authors would like to thank the following:

Mr and Mrs John Jervoise for their interest in this project and for giving permission to reproduce. documents from the Jervoise family archive.

Hampshire Archives Trust for a grant towards the cost of publication.

Hampshire Record Office staff for their help with the illustrations.

Barry Clarke, Botanist at Sir Harold Hillier Gardens, Romsey, for advice on plant name changes.

Brent Elliott, Historian at RHS Lindley Library, London, for suggestions for further reading.

David Standing, former Head Gardener, and Keith Oakley, present Gardener, at The Wakes, Selborne, for information about 18th-century vegetables and the growing methods used by Gilbert White.

Jane Davies for transcribing Repton's letters and other documents.

Dr Sally Jeffery for information about John James and George London at Herriard.

Deborah Markham and the Odiham Society for information about John Armstrong.

Susan Campbell for reading our text and for permission to reproduce plates from her book *A History of Kitchen Gardening*.

Copyright © Hampshire Gardens Trust 2019

Hampshire Gardens Trust

Registered charity no. 289378
Jermyns Lane
Romsey
Hampshire SO51 0QA
Website: www.hgt.org.uk
Email: admin@hgt.org.uk

www.hampshirearchivestrust.co.uk

Published with the support of a grant from Hampshire Archives Trust

Text copyright © Sally Miller, Sheila Carey-Thomas, Dee Clift & Eleanor Waterhouse 2019

Sally Miller, Sheila Carey-Thomas, Dee Clift & Eleanor Waterhouse have asserted their rights to be identified as authors of this work in accordance with the Copyright, Designs and Patents Act, 1988.

All rights reserved. No part of this publication may be reproduced, stored in a retrieval system, or transmitted, in any form or by any means, electronic or mechanical, by photocopying, recording or otherwise, without prior permission in writing from the publisher.

A CIP catalogue record for this book is available from the British Library.

ISBN-13: 978-1-9161901-0-8

Editor: Sue Gordon
Designer: Steve Cluett

Printed and bound in Hampshire using materials accredited by the Forest Stewardship Council by SO23print.co.uk

Humphry Repton at Herriard Park

'Improving the Premises'

Sally Miller
with
Sheila Carey-Thomas, Dee Clift, Eleanor Waterhouse

Hampshire Gardens Trust

Contents

Preface — 5

Introduction — 7

George Purefoy Jervoise (1770–1847) — 9

Humphry Repton (1752–1818) — 13

Repton's relationship with his client — 15

The new Kitchen Garden — 20

The new planting — 25

A note about plant nurseries — 26

Fruit trees for the Kitchen Garden — 27

Vegetables for the Kitchen Garden — 31

Tree planting and hedge laying — 35

Plantations and Shrubberies — 38

Small flowering and ornamental plants — 45

Whose hand? — 49

John Armstrong, nurseryman (1758–1819) — 51

Postscript — 54

Notes — 56

Appendices — 61

Bibliography — 94

Picture credits — 96

Preface

The Jervoise family came into the estate of Herriard at the beginning of the 17th century and began to amass a huge archive of papers, never throwing away even the smallest scrap of a note or list. That archive contains one quarter of a million items. It is still the property of the owner of Herriard but is deposited at the Hampshire Record Office.

The aim of this research project by Hampshire Gardens Trust was to reconstruct the work carried out by George Purefoy Jervoise (1770–1847) at Herriard Park between 1793 and 1799 for a new walled kitchen garden, pleasure grounds and plantations to plans drawn up by the landscape gardener Humphry Repton (1752–1818). We know that Repton was paid for a Red Book for Herriard, but that is lost.[1] However, Repton's letters to his client survive, as do detailed bills. The invoices for construction and planting, which are part of the Jervoise family archive at Hampshire Record Office, have been transcribed and analysed. The result is a description of what was done at Herriard together with the scale and cost of the works. The research also revealed that much of the planting illustrates the principles Repton described in his several publications.

June 9. 1793.

Sir,

On monday next which will be the 17th instant, I hope to have the pleasure of meeting you at Herriard — but as I shall come from Berkshire & cannot exactly fix an hour I will not trouble you to send any one to direct me in the road, but will take some person from Basing stoke for that purpose — & I hope to be with you before 12 o'clock if possible —

I have the honour to be Sir,

Your most Obedient humble Servant
H. Repton

N.3. Cockspur Street —
I leave Town on Wednesday
& shall hardly be able to receive
any answer to this.

Introduction

On Friday 9 June 1793 Humphry Repton wrote to George Purefoy Jervoise from lodgings in London (3 Cockspur Street, off the Strand) to confirm a meeting at Herriard on 17 June '… but as I shall come from Berkshire & cannot exactly fix an hour, I will not trouble you to send anyone to meet me in the road.' He would find someone in Basingstoke to show him the way and hoped to be there before noon. He was on the wing: a postscript reads 'I leave town on Wednesday I shall hardly be able to receive any answer to this.'[2] [Fig. 1] The visit, of two days, took place as arranged, but on 6 September Repton wrote from Stoke Park, in Herefordshire, to apologize for the delay in fulfilling his undertaking to produce plans for Herriard.[3] Two letters from Jervoise had caught up with him at Stoke. He promised to complete the plans in September and could not resist adding 'I am at this very time refusing several great concerns in this county that I may get home to discharge my engagement with respect to Herriard.'[4]

How Repton was introduced to Jervoise is not known. But Jane Austen knew of Repton[5] and she knew the Jervoise family, writing of them in a letter to her sister dated January 1799.[6]

Herriard was Repton's first commission in Hampshire: his nearest commission prior to 1793 was in Sussex.[7] He had been in business as a 'landscape gardener' (a term he was the first to use as a professional title) for less than five years:

> I have adopted the term *'Landscape Gardening'* as the most proper, because art can only be advanced and perfected by uniting the powers of the landscape painter and the practical gardener. The former must conceive a plan, which the latter may be able to execute.[8]

At this stage in his career he was being seen – and positioned himself – as the natural successor to Lancelot 'Capability' Brown and was very much in vogue, so it seems likely that Jervoise wanted to engage him as a signal of his own fashionable credentials. The old gardens at Herriard, or what remained of them, were to be almost completely replaced by Repton's plans for a new Kitchen Garden, plantations and pleasure grounds.

Fig. 1 – Repton's first letter to his new client, George Purefoy Jervoise, dated 9 June 1793.

George Purefoy Jervoise (1770–1847)

Herriard Park lies between Basingstoke and Alton in the rolling downland of Hampshire between the 500ft and 700ft contours. [Fig. 2] It was owned by the Coudrey (Cowdray) family until the mid-16th century, when it was inherited by three sisters. One sister, Elizabeth, married Richard Paulet, youngest brother of Lord St John of Basing, subsequently first Marquess of Winchester. Richard Paulet acquired the shares of the other two sisters, and Herriard became part of the vast estates of the Paulet family, centred on their seat at Basing.[9] In 1601 Herriard passed to Lucy Paulet, married to Sir Thomas Jervoise (1587–1654), in which family it remains. One hundred years later, Sir Thomas's grandson, the third Thomas Jervoise, commissioned architect John James[10] to build a new mansion and George London to lay out formal gardens.[11] It was this house and garden that George Purefoy Jervoise inherited in 1792 from his childless uncle, Tristram Huddleston Jervoise. George Purefoy Jervoise was the son of the Revd George Huddleston Purefoy of Britford, in Wiltshire, and was the oldest of seven children.[12] He was educated at Westminster School and Oxford University – a classical education appropriate for an eldest son of country gentry. More importantly it would fit him for the higher social status he would enjoy as owner of Herriard. George lived at Herriard with his uncle before inheriting, and his uncle took a keen interest in his education, writing to him in 1785, when he (George) was 15:

> I hope you begin to relish Homer & that the Greek Language is become more easy to your faculties, tho' at your leisure hours I strongly recommend it to you to advert to the Mathematick which will eventually be exceeding useful to you in Life.[13]

The house George Purefoy Jervoise inherited had been built in 1704 in a restrained baroque style. [Fig. 3] A brick building of three storeys and basement, the front of nine bays, the sides of five. An unusual feature was that almost

Fig. 2 – Herriard Park, showing its relationship to Hackwood Park and Basing House. Detail from Isaac Taylor's one-inch map of Hampshire, 1759.

Fig. 3 – Architect's model of the house built in 1704.

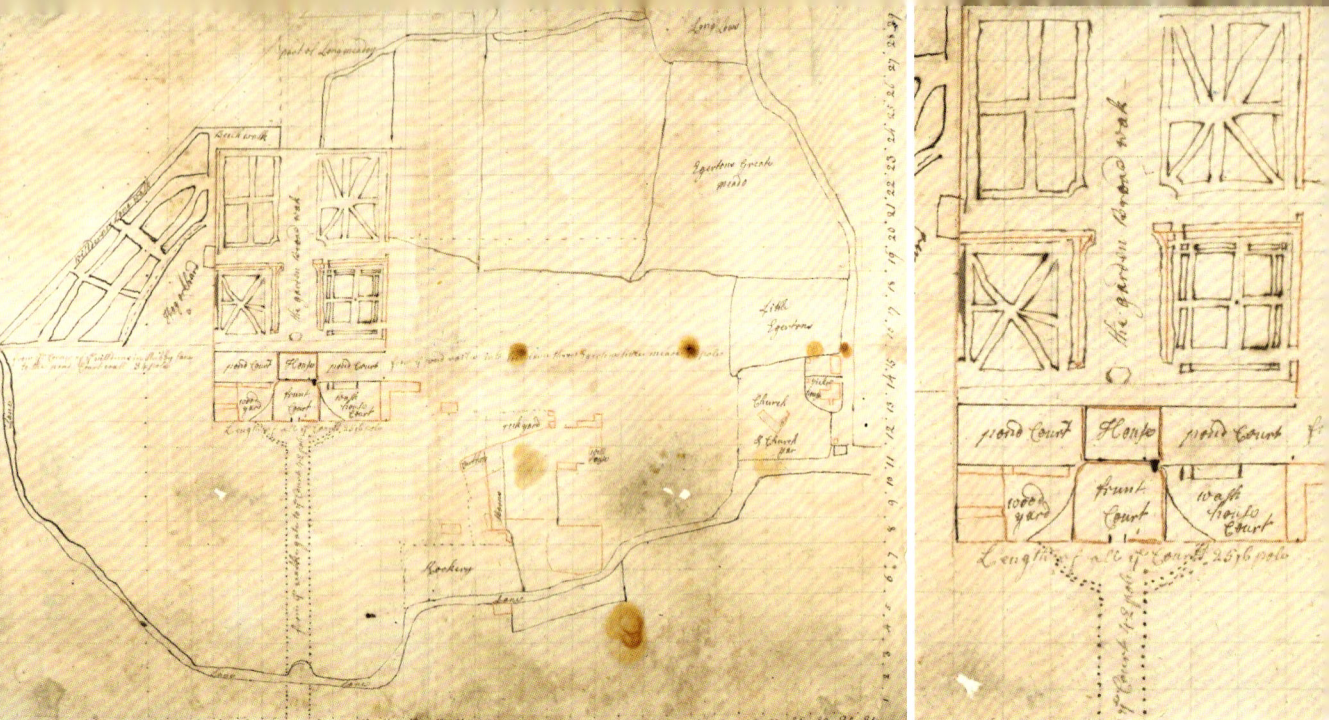

Fig. 4 – Sketch layout of the house and gardens at Herriard shortly after they were created c.1704.

Fig. 5 – Detail from Fig. 4 showing the house and its courts.

all service functions were contained in the basement, as was the practice in town houses.[14] That house stood until 1965, when it was replaced with the present, smaller house on the same site. A sketch map probably made by Thomas Jervoise, undated but pre-1707, shows the original house in relation to its approaches, the church and other buildings. [Fig. 4] Its walled entrance court conceals on one side the Wood Yard and, on the other, the Wash House Court, but there is no additional range of service buildings. [Fig.5] By the time Jervoise inherited, this layout of walled courtyards would have felt old fashioned, as would the house with its wainscoted and panelled rooms.

Likewise, the gardens were little changed from those designed and planted by George London as the setting for the house. The house is flanked by two Pond Courts, beyond which a terrace on the garden front opens a view down a Broad Walk flanked by four parterres. To one side there is an Orchard, a Wilderness of walks through a small wood and a Beech Walk. There is no walled Kitchen Garden, but we know from archive evidence that the two quarters farthest from the house were used to grow fruit and vegetables.[15] It was a modest country house garden, and this sketch probably shows what was created, although the beautiful plans by George London dated 1699 show a rather more elaborate layout of the parterres. London's plan shows a greenhouse at the eastern end of the cross walk separating the formal parterres from the quarters for 'Kitchin Stuff'. [Fig. 6] The glasshouse is marked but not named in the sketch map. George Purefoy Jervoise was only 23 years old when he commissioned Humphry

Fig. 6 – George London's elaborate design for pond courts and garden parterres at Herriard, dated 1699.

Fig. 7 – 'Herriard House, the seat of George Purefoy Jervoise Esq.' Lithograph, G.F. Prosser, n.d. but *c*.1830.

Repton and started to spend very large sums of money on improvements at Herriard. The old formal garden with its ponds and parterres must have been erased at this time. No trace of it remains except a level area south of the modern house, below the terrace.[16]

Many of Repton's commissions included building a new house or modifying an existing one, but this was not the case at Herriard.[17] However, Jervoise set about modernizing the old house, employing a vast array of craftsmen and buying or commissioning a great deal of furniture and fashionable interior décor items. The expenditure increased dramatically on his marriage in 1798 to Elizabeth Hall (1771–1821), daughter and sole heir of Thomas Hall of the neighbouring parish of Preston Candover. By 1799 Jervoise calculated that he had spent the enormous sum of £5,185 on the house alone, and between 1792 and 1799 about 30 per cent of his total expenditure went on 'fitting up Herriard House in rendering it habitable, and by the improvement of the Premises contiguous to the Mansion, and of the future benefit of the estate'. He later regretted his rashness, admitting that he had been struck by 'the idea of partaking of immediate gratification'.[18] [Fig. 7] Converting historic monetary values to present-day values is tricky, but a conversion based on income or wealth value of sterling suggests that £5,185 represents almost half a million pounds today.[19]

Humphry Repton (1752–1818)

Fig. 8 – Humphry Repton by Henry Bryan Hall.

Humphry Repton was born in Bury St Edmond's, Suffolk, eldest son of a Collector of Excise with small land holdings. The family moved to Norwich and in 1764, when Humphry was 12 years old, his father sent him to Holland to learn Dutch in order to fit him to become a merchant in the prosperous textile trade between East Anglia and Holland. In Rotterdam he lodged with a rich merchant banker – a formative experience as he there learnt to mix with and enjoy the company of those of a higher social standing. He acquired valuable social skills – dancing at balls, singing and playing his flute at musical evenings, sketching people and places – and the desire to enjoy the social life that shaped the rest of his life and his eventual career. Returning to Norwich, he was apprenticed at the age of 16 to a textile merchant.

When Humphry married in 1773, his father set him up in the textile business, but he was no businessman and his heart was not in it. The death of both parents released him from the family obligation and, with a modest inheritance, he moved his young family to Susted Old Hall, in Norfolk. It had a small farm attached, and Repton set about enjoying the life of a gentleman farmer. But, with a family of 16 children in all (only seven survived infancy), the need to find a regular source of income became pressing. In 1786 they left Susted and settled in a small cottage in the village of Hare Street, in Essex, nearer to London and potential employment. Humphry's writing and sketching skills gave him some work in the theatre and publishing worlds, but it was not enough and in 1788 he recorded that he woke one morning with a new profession clear in his mind, one that would combine his love of the natural world with his skills in writing and sketching. He immediately set about writing to all his acquaintances, explaining his intention of becoming a 'Landscape Gardener'. He was excited and, as always, optimistic. [Fig. 9]

> Now at the age of 36 years – I commence a new career … I boldly venture forth once more, and with renewed energy and hope push off my little bark into a sea unknown.[20]

Repton never grew rich like Brown, but by 1790 he was making a modest income. In 1793 war broke out with France and was to continue for the rest of his working life. It blighted his career. Also, however, the society in which he had been so comfortable was changing fast. The wealthy were less inclined to spend money on improving their properties; income tax had been introduced for the first time to pay for the wars; and inflation was rising. Repton's fees for visits had always included time on the road but by 1806, he charged 70 guineas for visits at 140 miles from London; 50 guineas at 100 miles and so on down a scale to 10 guineas within a stage (generally 10 to 15 miles) of London.

The income tax introduced by Prime Minister Pitt outraged him: 'Now I must abide by this', he wrote to his son, 'or kick the Commissioners or bid them kiss my A.'[21]

Very few Repton-designed landscapes have survived: the changes he proposed were often subtle and on a small scale, quickly superseded by later designs and planting. He realized later in his career that his writings on landscape gardening would be the more important part of his legacy. He published *Sketches and Hints on Landscape Gardening* in 1795; *Observations on the Theory and Practice of Landscape Gardening* in 1803, and in 1806 he recycled parts of both in a cheaper volume intended for a wider audience, *An Enquiry into the Changes of Taste in Landscape Gardening*. In 1808 he produced sumptuous plans for the Brighton Pavilion, for which he was not paid when the Prince of Wales dropped the plans in favour of those by Nash. He tried to salvage something from that huge disappointment by publishing *Designs for the Pavilion at Brighton*. In 1811 injuries sustained in an overturned carriage accident confined him to a wheelchair for most of the rest of his life. He was no longer easily able to visit land-owning clients across the country, and his last commissions were for smaller scale gardens within reach of home.

Fig. 9 – Repton's business card for his new profession of 'Landscape Gardener', depicting him as a man of action with his theodolite. Thomas Medland (1765–1833).

Repton's relationship with his client

Following his visit to Herriard in June 1793, Repton despatched the plans on 27 September, as he had promised:

> Sir, I have this day sent to London a parcel to be forwarded by the coach to Basingstoke which I hope you will receive safe – but as I have once lost such a parcel by the carelessness of the coachman I will beg the favor of you to write to me when you have received it.

He went on to solicit 'your approbation of my labours', said that he would be in the neighbourhood of Reading about the end of October and could continue 'to Herriards if you will have the goodness to let me know whether I can be of any use to you this year'.

1793 June 17th. & 18th.	
First visit 2 days	£10: 10: 0
Expense of Journey	£5: 5: 0
Red Book of Plans etc	£21: 0: 0
Dec 3rd. One day & Expenses	£8: 8: 0
Dec 9th Working Plan instructions for Kitchen Garden & Plantations	£ 1: 1: 0
	£46: 4: 0
1793 Dec 3rd. Rec'd on account	
	£10: 10: 0
	£35: 14: 0

The parcel that Repton refers to was the Red Book for Herriard Park, and his bill for it has survived.[22] [Fig. 10] There are two slips of paper attached to this document, both in Repton's

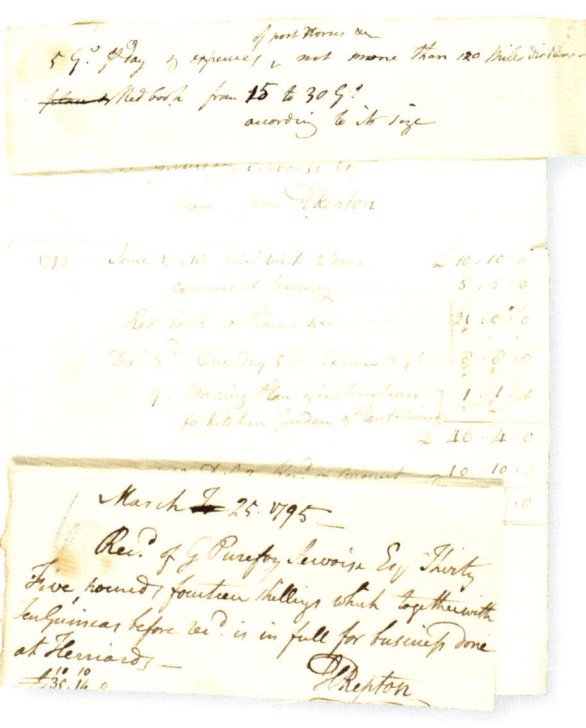

Fig. 10 – Repton's 1793 bill to George Purefoy Jervoise, showing two attached slips of paper.

hand. The first, a scrawled note, possibly given to Jervoise on the first visit: '5 G [guineas] per day of expenses for post horses not more than 120 Miles Return. Red Book from 15 to 30 G according to its size.'[23]

The second slip attached to the bill is dated 25 March 1795: 'Rec'd of G. Purefoy Jervoise Esq. Thirty Five pounds fourteen shillings which together with the Ten Guineas before rec'd is in full for business done at Herriards. [signed] H Repton.'

The £21 for the Herriard Red Book would represent over £2,000 in purchasing power today. The first Red Book that Repton produced was for Brandsbury, in Middlesex, in 1789 and he charged 10 guineas for it. The second, in the same year, for Thomas Coke of Holkham, was a gift.

As Repton's business grew, the time-consuming labour of making these books became more onerous: by 1792 he had already prepared over one hundred.[24] But they were his trademark and clients expected them, so his charges increased over time and he never again gave one as a gift.[25] In 1790 Repton charged 2 guineas a day for work carried out at home, so the Herriard Red Book would have taken up to ten days to complete.

The Red Books are Repton's lasting artistic legacy and were the perfect expression of his style. Sketches of the 'unimproved' landscape were overlaid with hinged slides that could be lifted to reveal the Reptonian transformation. The accompanying discursive and flattering text was handwritten in elegant copperplate. Repton rarely drew plans, only sketching what would be seen if the improvements he recommended were carried out.

As he began work at Herriard, this approach was already the subject of amused comment among the watching cognoscenti, as in this letter written in 1794 from William Mason to William Gilpin:

Repton a successor to Mr Brown very much in vogue can draw in your way very freely, which Brown could not do in any way. By this means he alters places on Paper and makes them so picturesque that fine folks think that all the oaks etc. he draws on paper will grow exactly in the shape and fashion in which he delineated them, so they employ him at a great Price; so much the better on both sides, for they might lay out their money far worse and he has a numerous family of children to bring up.[26]

Repton positioned himself as a consultant and that was the flaw in his business plan. Unlike Brown, he was not a contractor – which was where the money was to be made. Some clients paid for a Red Book simply to have an album of views to display in their libraries; others ignored or altered his proposals or implemented them piecemeal using their own labour.

On 22 October 1793 Repton returned home from a visit to Northamptonshire to find another letter from Jervoise, requesting his presence at Herriard the following Sunday. He replied:

I will make a forced march to reach
Basingstoke on Sunday evening & Herriards
before nine on Monday morning the 28th ...
that I might have the pleasure of conferring
with you on the spot before you leave it.
I wish it had been in my power to come one
day sooner, but it is with much difficulty
that I shall be able to accomplish what
I have promised.

However, Repton immediately fell ill (a
'nervous disorder') and was unable to keep
his appointment at Herriard. In his letter of
apology he asks 'if you will explain by letter
the nature of the departure from the plan –
I shall perhaps be able to answer you on paper.'
So within a month of receiving the Red Book,
Jervoise was already making changes to the plans.

By the end of November Repton was fit to
travel. He wrote that he would be in the
neighbourhood of Reading, and offered to
run over on a convenient day. He could be
contacted under cover to the Rt Hon. the
Speaker[27] at Woodley, near Reading, where he
would be staying.[28] He signed the receipt for
ten guineas on account, dated 3 December
1793, which implies the visit took place.

From this point on his relationship with this
client appears to stagnate. On 1 January
1794 he writes to ask if Jervoise had received
safe in London the plan for the Kitchen
Garden & Plantations, which he had sent on
9 December last. The letter also presented
again his unpaid bill from 1793. [Fig. 10].
In November 1794 he writes to say he will again
be at the Speaker's house, 'from where I have
generally cros'd [sic] over to Herriard House ...
if you wish'd me to see the progress you have
made since my last visit I might avail myself
of this opportunity.' There is no evidence he
visited at this time, and on 1 January 1795 he
was chasing his bill, still unpaid. He was finally
paid the balance of £35 14s 0d on 25 March
1795 and signed for it, but there is no record of
a visit on this date, so it is possible the money
was transferred to him via a bank in London
and the receipt sent back to Herriard.[29] An
estate book-keeping entry dated 25 March 1795
for 'Improving of the Premises at Herriards
Park' confirms 'Mr Repton's bill £46: 4: 0',
for 'laying out the Plantations'.[30]

In June 1795 Repton wrote to say that he would
be at Woodley again and 'when I can be of any
service at Herriard I shall be happy to pay my
respects to you if you will have the goodness
to write to me'. It seems a visit was arranged,
and on 15 July Repton wrote that he had fixed
his route to reach Basingstoke by the evening
of 20 July. 'I will therefore have the pleasure of
waiting on you at Herriards house on Tuesday
morning the 21st.'

In early 1796 there was confusion over
arrangements for another visit. Repton was to
be in Winchester and offered to visit Herriard
on Thursday 21 January but he had another
engagement near Windsor to fit in. Jervoise

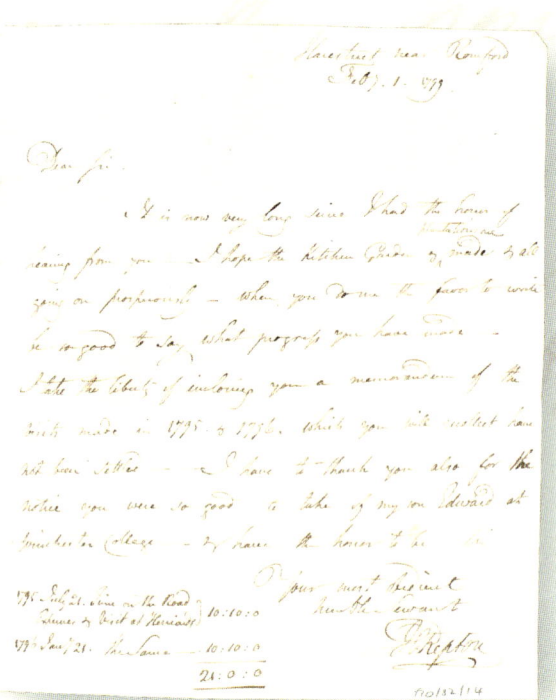

Fig. 11 – Repton's letter of February 1799, with his final bill.

must have asked him to visit on 22 January instead as Repton replied 'in my former letter I had requested that favour [of a visit] for the 21st as I am under the necesity [*sic*] of being in Winchester on the morning of the 22nd.' He hoped that the 21st would be equally convenient and offered to be at Herriards as soon after 10.00 as possible.

There is then an interval in the letters before Repton writes again to Jervoise in February 1799. [Fig.11, transcribed below] This letter is clearly an attempt to renew communication with his client – and chase payment of his outstanding bill. The memorandum in the bottom left corner of the letter confirms Repton's previous two visits, each of one day.

Dear Sir
It is now very long since I had the honour of hearing from you – I hope the Kitchen Garden & Plantations are made [and] all going on propitiously – when you do me the favour to write be so good to say what progress you have made – I take the liberty of inclosing you a memorandum of visits made in 1795 & 1796, which you will recollect have not been settled – I have to thank you also for the notice you were so good to take of my son Edward at Winchester College – & have the honor to be, Sir, your most obedient humble servant, [signed] H Repton.

REPTON AT HERRIARD PARK   18   IMPROVING THE PREMISES

1795	July 21. Time on the Road	
	Expenses & visit at Herriards	10:10:0
1796	Jan 21. The same	10:10:0
		21: 0: 0

An estate account document under the heading 'Mr Repton'[31] lists a payment of £21 in 1798, which probably is settlement for the visits in 1795 & 1796. However, Jervoise was building new stables at Herriard in 1798/99 and another set of accounts details 'Expenses applicable to the Improvements of Herriard Premises. Building of Kitchen Garden Wall … Building of stables', and includes '1799 Dec 28th. Mr Repton's Account £26 - -'.[32] This may have been either a final accounting for bills outstanding or a further bill. The only confirmed visits Repton made to Herriard were in 1793 (three days), 1795 (one day) and 1796 (one day). The 1796 visit was in January: the first brick for the new kitchen garden he had designed was laid on 31 March that year, so Repton never saw the kitchen garden he had designed.

The letter of 1799 seems to mark the end of Repton's involvement at Herriard. There is one final letter in the archive, dated 13 April 1801. Repton wrote that he would shortly be in the neighbourhood and 'I am unwilling to be so near Herriards without giving you notice of it that I may have the pleasure of paying my respects to you, if I can be of any use to finish the plans for improvement begun under my directions.' But there is no evidence that he visited then.

What these letters illustrate is how persistent Repton was in cultivating a client, although Herriard was not a large commission for him. An important aspect of his chosen profession was the opportunity to mix with and be accepted by his social superiors.[33] 'The chief benefit I have derived from it has been the society of those to whose notice I could not otherwise have aspired.'[34]

In this respect his ambitions reflect those of his client. Jervoise had through inheritance acquired a life that he acknowledged had always been his father's ambition for him. He enjoyed it and spent money on Herriard to signal and cement his new standing in the social order.[35]

The new Kitchen Garden

The first brick of the walls for the new kitchen garden was laid on 31 March 1796 by G.P. Jervoise and the 35 persons present were recorded. The list is revealingly domestic: Lawyer; Senior Steward; Housekeeper; Butler; Senior Groom; Gardener; Housemaid; Carpenters, Plumbers, Bricklayers; Plaisterers [sic]; Cordwainer; Woodmen; Labourers, all named.[36] [Fig. 12]

An estimate for the construction is in the archive:[37]

An estimate of Brick, Lime & Sand for the Garden Walls supposed to take 146,000 of old Brick to raise the foundation 2 ft. above Ground & it will require 172,000 to make the walls 10ft high & the back wall 12ft. with flues of new Bricks.

It will take 70 Loads of Lime & about 105 Loads of Sand

New Bricks & carriage	£322: 10: 0
Lime & carriage	80: 0: 0
Sand & carriage	73: 10: 0
Building the Walls	95: 4: 0
Cleaning & Moving Old Bricks	14: 12: 0
Diging [sic] out the foundation	2: 2: 6
	£587: 18: 6

The very detailed accounts in the archive for the construction of the garden walls include some 'double accounting', which had to be identified and stripped out. The analysis is set out in Appendix 1. In 1796, when the bulk of the building work took place, the cost of purchasing and delivering the building materials was £630 15s 7½d. The actual cost for labourers at Herriard in 1796 was £150, almost double that for the previous year, so a good proportion of them must have been engaged in 'Building the Walls'.[38]

Another series of accounts, 'Expenses attending the New Kitchen garden Walls, Green House', lists expenses dated 1796–1800 for bricks, carriage of lime and sand, stonemason, slater, glazier, painter, plumber, carpenter, sawyer, annotated in pencil with the total £991: 19: 4 ¼.[39] In 1799 Jervoise sent his father an 'Account of Receipts & Disbursements from 1792 to 1799' where he lists 'New Kitchen Garden £1000' (as a project cost; over £93,000 today).[40]

Repton designed several walled kitchen gardens and had firm views about positioning, layout and usage, detailed in his various publications. The earliest complete plan of the Herriard kitchen garden is on a 'Plan of the Garden and Shrubberies' dated 1818. [Fig. 13] It is not

Fig. 12 – 'A List of Persons present at the laying of the first Brick of Herriard Garden Walls, 31st March 1796.'

A List of Persons present at laying the first Brick of Herriard Garden Wall March 31, 1796

G. P. Jervoise Esqr. Proprietor
Revd. I. P. Jervoise
Richd. Fry, Senior — Steward
Joseph Turpin. Woodman of Lasham
Mr. Jones Carpenter & Surveyor
Mr. Glover Plumber
Geo. Mountford Butler to G. P. Jervoise Esqr.
Saml. Lee Senr. Groom — Do.
Thos. Barndall Senr. Bricklayer
Saml. Lee Junr. Footman G. P. Jervoise Esqr.
Edmd. Redding — Carpenter
Joshr. Stroud — Sawyer
Robt. Love
Patrick McCartey } Plaisterers
Inr. Douty
Wm. Henness Gardener
Lydia Fry House-maid — G. P. Jervoise Esqr.
Thos. Barndall Junr. Brick-layer
Thos. Pierce — Carpenter
Inr. Trouting — Do.
Charles Parris — Do.
Thos. Gardener — Do.
Wm. Freeborne — Cordwainer
Mrs. Fry — Housekeeper — G. P. Jervoise Esqr.
Joshua Goodall Labourer
John Fry Junr. } Sons of Richd. Fry. Steward
Richd. Fry Junr.
Wm. Paine Bricklayer

Wm. Wooton — Labourer to Bricklayer
Inr. Culley Bricklayer
Wm. Wood
Wm. Stroud — Bricklayers Labourer
Joshr. Gearle — Bricklayer
Richd. Grantham — Carter
Stephr. Pierce — Labourer

21

THE NEW KITCHEN GARDEN

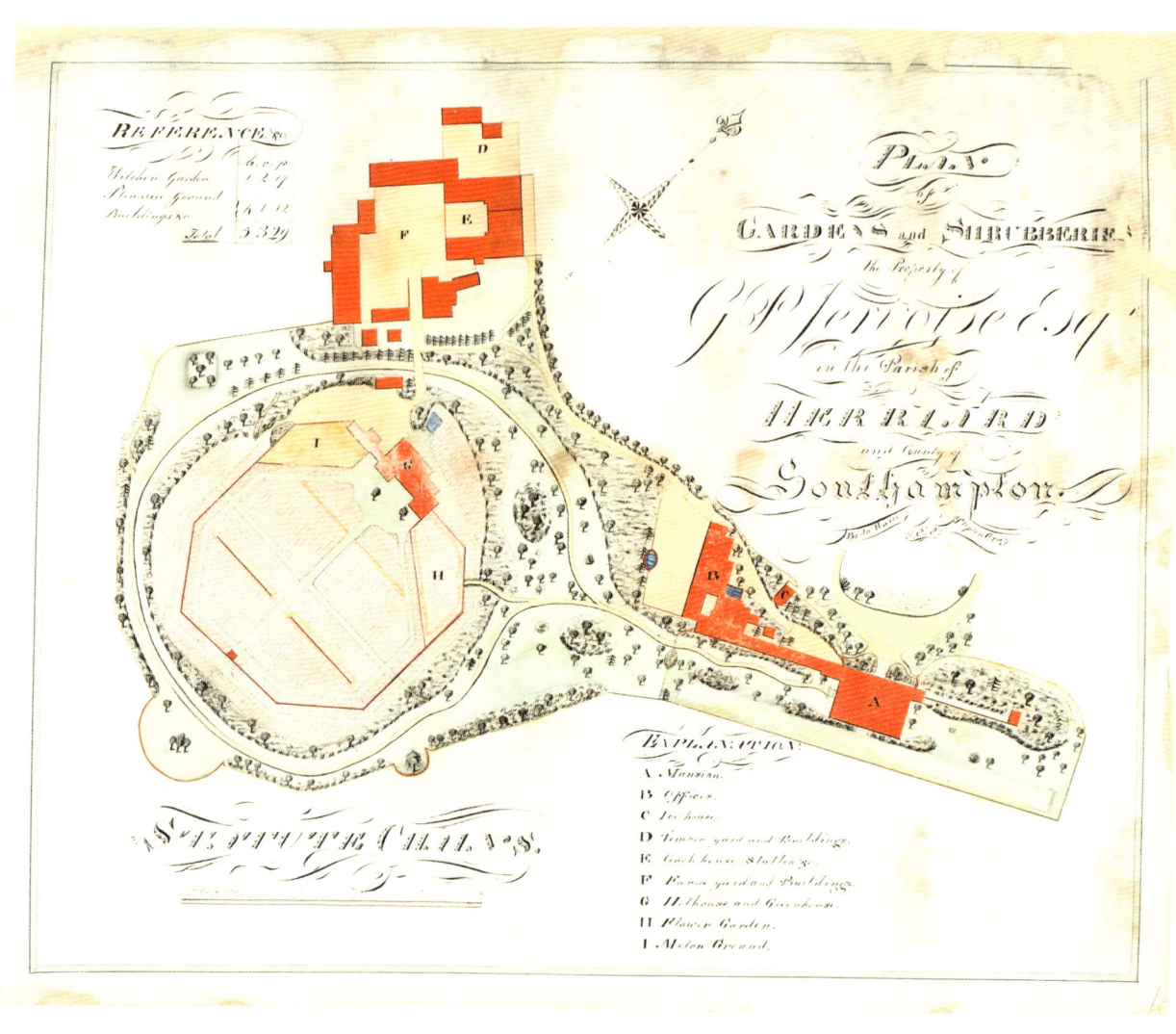

Fig. 13 – 'Plan of Gardens and Shrubberies' – the earliest complete plan of the kitchen garden designed by Repton, dated 1818.

known why a plan was made in that year. It was possibly connected with a revision of wills and inheritance: Jervoise's father-in-law died in 1812 and his estates passed to the Jervoises. They had no surviving children and Herriard passed to George's sister upon his death in 1847.[41] But the title of the plan is in itself significant. Repton consistently referred to it as a kitchen garden and, as can be seen, the plan is filled by this practical space. To quote from Nicola Pink, 'Clearly the unfashionable word 'kitchen' has been deliberately dropped in favour of the more fashionable 'shrubbery', which brings to mind leisure rather than unpleasant toil. The move away from language associated with work could be seen here as a clear class statement implying that the Jervoises are a people of pleasure and ease.'[42]

The Herriard kitchen garden is octagonal and oriented slightly north-east to south-west, and it encloses approximately two hectares. Octagonal and hexagonal walled gardens have several advantages over square or rectangular ones. It had been known for a long time that the orientation of walls was a critical factor in protecting plants and enhancing their productivity. Lancelot 'Capability' Brown designed hexagonal kitchen gardens (at least three) as well as three octagonal kitchen gardens, including a very large one at Luton Hoo, in Bedfordshire, completed in 1770 for John Stuart 3rd Earl of Bute, a keen and knowledgeable horticulturist and botanist who had very precise requirements.[43] Repton would have known about Brown's innovation and followed him by designing hexagonal or octagonal kitchen gardens himself at three sites in addition to Herriard.[44]

At Luton Hoo, the sun's rays fall on the north-west wall at sunrise and the south-east wall at sunset. At the equinoxes in March and September they fall on the east and west walls respectively.[45] The Herriard kitchen garden is orientated in the same way. The estimate specifies that the walls be 10ft high, the usual height at this time, although the 'back wall' (the north wall) is to be 12ft 'with flues of new bricks' to heat the hothouse and greenhouse. These would have been 'lean-to' constructions against the back wall. The tax on glass was not abolished until 1845, so greenhouses before that point rarely had more than one front wall of glass. The references to 'Cleaning and Moving Old Bricks' suggests there may have been a previous kitchen garden or buildings, demolished to make way for the new garden, possibly on the same site.

The 1818 plan shows a melon ground (I) to one side of the hothouse and greenhouse. This would have contained the hot beds and pits in which the melons and cucumbers were grown. Within the walls, the garden is divided by two more transverse walls to maximize the opportunities for growing wall fruit. The 'Flower garden' (H) and the perimeter and transverse walks are typical Repton features. The plan shows a walk from the house entering directly into the flower garden, allowing the owner to avoid the main entrance opposite the stables. Repton often advised that small flower gardens, regularly planted (what we might now call a cutting

Fig. 14 – Aerial photograph of the walls of the kitchen garden, which have survived intact.

garden), be placed in front of a greenhouse or orangery, secluded from the general scenery and so distinct from the more informal planting of shrubberies outside the walls.[46]

A working kitchen garden was a convenience, not an ornament, but Repton wanted it to be arranged for pleasure as well as profit. Winter walks might be made in its warmth and shelter. And, even where there were no hothouses, in the south border early flowers and vegetables would be cheering. In summer, when the walks within the walls could be very hot, he advised training fruit trees on hoops over the walks to make shady alleys, 'from whence the apples, pears, and plums are seen hanging within our reach; and grapes so trained will sometimes ripen without artificial heat.' Further, these shaded walks would surround and enclose the quarters devoted to the more mundane garden crops, 'which, well managed, will scarcely be visible from the walks; and a screen of gooseberries, currants, raspberries, and asparagus beds, surrounding these, will make a cheerful blind during a great part of the summer months.'[47]

The walls of the Herriard kitchen garden exist intact, but the garden itself has been re-purposed. Some surviving planting around it and in the park is reminiscent of Repton's style. [Fig. 14]

The new planting

It is clear from our analysis that whoever was ordering the new planting at Herriard was knowledgeable about and interested in the newer and more exotic trees and plants then being raised in England. For the previous half century the eastern and south-eastern seaboard of North America had been yielding a wealth of new and exciting plants, and many feature as specimen plants, ordered in ones and twos for Herriard. While there are frequent bulk orders for unspecified 'evergreen and flowering shrubs', there are also orders for named trees, shrubs, fruit trees. Towards the end of the century new genera from the Cape began to be available, and these too figure in the Herriard lists.

In the list of those present at the laying of the first brick for the kitchen garden, there is one gardener, named as William Henness, but he does not appear anywhere else in the archive. Jervoise's Steward Richard Fry was, among other duties, in charge of managing the woodland and park. But a key figure is surely John Armstrong, who had a nursery at North Warnborough, about 5 miles from Herriard. He supplied all the trees, plants and seeds for Herriard from 1793 onwards (and probably before). It is not possible that he could supply all the orders – many of which were for unusual or exotic species – from his rural nursery, so he must have been buying some stock from the larger specialist commercial nurseries, probably those in west London. It is clear from the bills that he was earning substantial sums each year. Further, it is clear from mentions in Richard Fry's letters to Jervoise that he was also working at Herriard, perhaps as a contractor:

> Mr Armstrong was here on Wednesday last when he has sett [sic] out to begin taking up & transplanting your fir and other Trees beginning of next week and to continue the planting as fast as possible.[48]

Planting of all kinds continued from 1794 to 1800, peaking in 1796: native woodland trees; evergreens; ornamental and specimen trees; shrubs and perennials for the pleasure grounds; tender plants for the greenhouse; orchard top fruit; stone and soft fruits and desirable vegetables for forcing in the kitchen garden.

A note about plant nurseries

Up until the 18th century there were probably no more than 1,000 exotic (that is, non-native or naturalized) plant species available to the garden owner. During that century 5,000 more were introduced, the number accelerating as the century progressed and doubling between 1731 and 1768.[49]

Most of the important nurseries were located in or near London, the largest concentration in the second half of the 18th century being in west London along the three main roads that led out of the city through the villages of Kensington, Hammersmith and Chelsea. It is likely that Armstrong sourced many of his orders from these nurseries. The notable ones were Reginald Whitley's Old Brompton Nursery; Grimwood & Co, in Kensington; the Vineyard Nursery at Hammersmith founded by Lewis Kennedy and James Lee; and James Colville on The King's Road, Chelsea. All specialized in the exotic trees, shrubs and plants from the eastern seaboard of America and those newly arriving from the Cape of Good Hope. Some were imported from collectors in America, and the Vineyard sent out its own collectors. All developed expertise in propagating and growing the new arrivals. James Lee is famous for reportedly buying a previously unknown plant in a pot from a sailor's wife in Wapping. It was *Fuchsia coccinea* from Chile and it was said that Lee raised 300 cuttings from the one plant and sold them, well grown, at one guinea each.[50] It was the custom for nurserymen – or their agents – to visit customers once a year to collect orders and debts. But they also depended on the catalogues they published, the books they wrote and personal recommendation. Some of the catalogues at this time were works of art. [Fig. 15]

Fig. 15 – Display of fruits for August 1732, from *Twelve Months of Flowers*, advertisements produced by Robert Furber, nurseryman.

Fruit trees for the Kitchen Garden

No sooner had the Herriard kitchen garden walls been completed than very large numbers of fruit trees were ordered. In 1795 an order was made for just 12 standard almond trees, two dwarf apricots and one dwarf peach; in 1796 400 standard and dwarf fruit trees were ordered; and a further 108 in 1797. Just one order dated 31 October 1796 totalled £12 2s 6d for 199 plants: peaches, nectarines, apricots, cherries, figs, vines and currants. Vines and figs were 9d each, but peaches and nectarines ranged in cost from 2s 0d to 6s 0d each for 'dwarf, train'd' specimens. [Fig. 16]

Oct. 31 To 19 Dwarf Cherries 14 – 3
5 Dwarf Do. Train'd 15
2 Stand.d Do 2
15 Dwarf Pears 15
25 Dwarf Plumbs 18 – 9
9 Dwarf Apricots 9
15 Dwarf French Peaches 1 – 10
9 Dwarf Peaches 9
12 Dwarf Nectarines 12
1 Dwarf Fairchilds Do 2
1 Dwarf White Do 2
5 Stand.d Do 10
7 Stand.d Peaches 14
2 Figgs 1. 6
4 Vines in Pots 6
1 Do not in Pot 9
2 Stand.d Nectarines Train'd 10
3 Stand.d Peaches Do 15
7 Dwarf Do Do 1 – 15
2 Dwarf Nectarines Do 12
55 Currants 13. 3

Fig. 16 – List of the fruit trees and bushes ordered on 31 October 1796.

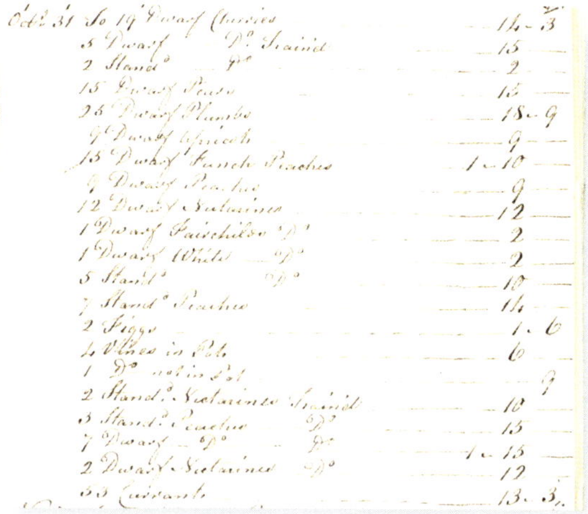

The orders dwindled to 76 total between 1798 and 1800, and some of those may have been replacements for failed plantings. The full list is at Appendix 2.

Many kinds of fruit, both hardy and tender, were grown: apples, pears, plums, cherries, nectarines, peaches and apricots feature in the lists. Interestingly, it is the more exotic and desirable dessert fruits, especially nectarines and peaches, that are ordered as named varieties; desirable because they were newly introduced or of the finest flavour and appearance. When served to guests they would enhance Jervoise's status. Apples, pears, plums are rarely ordered as named varieties: it may be that Armstrong, or the supplying nursery, already knew what would be needed or would grow well at Herriard. Standard fruit trees of every kind were ordered and many of those must have been orchard-planted.

Much fruit was grown against the walls of the kitchen garden, both inside and out. It was important to maximize production in the precious microclimate inside, and gardeners had become adept at different growing methods. The trees ordered for Herriard were specified as either 'standards' or 'dwarfs'. Standard trees could be either wall-grown or free-standing but, as the lists do not indicate how they were grown, we can only use contemporary references as a guide. The usual system of growing in the 18th century was to alternate dwarf trees, such as fans against

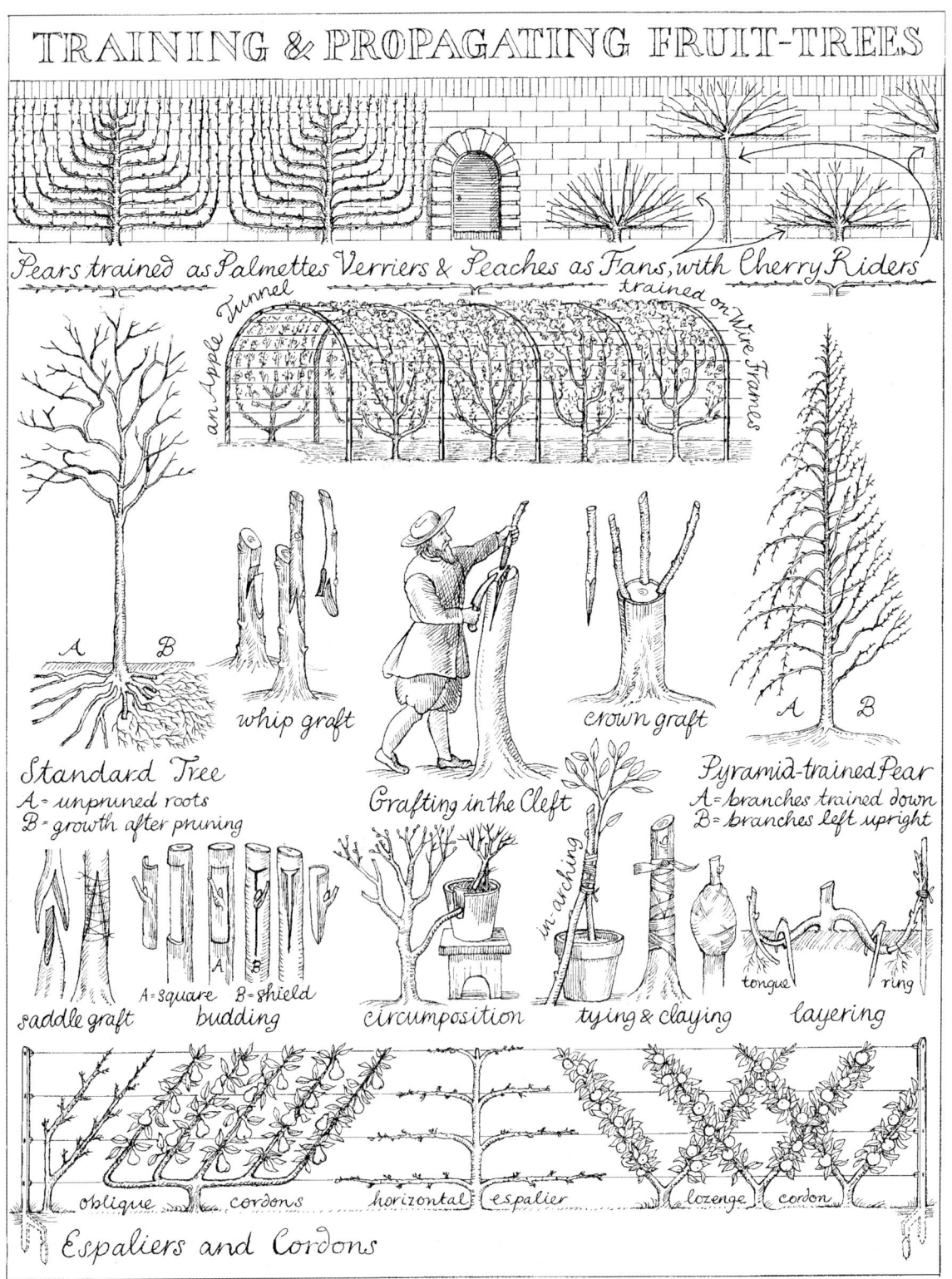

the walls, with standards. Philip Miller in *The Gardeners Dictionary* of 1769 advises planting espaliers and dwarfs between the standards against a wall:

> While the Dwarfs are filling the Bottom of the Walls, the Standards will cover the Tops, and will produce a great deal of Fruit; but these, as the Dwarfs arise to fill the Walls, must be cut away to make room for them; and when the Dwarf trees cover the Walls, the Standards should be intirely [*sic*] taken away. But I would advise, never to plant Standard cherries over other Fruits; for there is no other Sort of Fruit that will prosper well under the Drip of Cherries.[51]

Some dwarfs were also grown as cordons or espaliers. These created 'pole hedges' against the walls, and did not need walls as tall as those required by many standards. These dwarf trees were small enough to be planted closely together on a wall, and so could be easily protected by coverings when necessary from frost and poor weather. They were created either by 'heading down', or severe pruning, or by grafting the desired variety on to the rootstock of a low-growing tree. They were a very productive method of growing. In her *History of Kitchen Gardening* Susan Campbell explains that dwarf trees originated in France, the French having developed the art of growing tender fruits such as apricots, peaches and almonds a century before.[52] [Fig. 17]

Dwarf trees of more native varieties such as cherries, pears, plums and apples were also ordered. These were not tender fruit so would not need protection, but when grown as dwarfs they fruited earlier than standards, so increased productivity. It was also found that dwarf trees grew bigger in the wetter English climate and also they were not as long-lived as standards. Through the 18th century there was much experimenting with spacing and 'companion' grouping of dwarf and standard trees.[53]

Gilbert White, when planting his new fruit wall at Selborne in 1761, alternated his peaches, nectarines and apricots with vines, to grow up and round to protect this precious crop. This does not appear to be the case at Herriard, but this was common practice and it may be that standards such as cherries and plums were used in much the same way.

The lists do not tell us which fruit was planted inside the walls and which outside, but all the nectarines, four peaches and two cherries were ordered as 'trained', which must be an indicator of location inside the walls.

Fig. 17 – Drawings showing methods of training and propagating for fruit trees.

FRUIT TREES FOR THE KITCHEN GARDEN

rather than for fruit production, so these were perhaps intended to enhance the attractiveness of the orchard in spring.

Only in 1797 was a great deal of soft fruit ordered: strawberries, raspberries and gooseberries. It is interesting that, although no variety of the 1,550 strawberry plants was specified, the 239 raspberries were all 'cane', 'white', 'Antwerp' or 'nettlestrips', and of the 68 gooseberries 48 were 'Lancashire'. Jervoise married in 1798 and we can speculate that perhaps his bride had a particular fondness for soft fruits. There are odd omissions from the lists: only two fig trees and one olive and, most notably, no pineapples, at that time the most luxurious and expensively raised fruit you could put on your table.

There were gifts too:

Fig. 18 – The Nut Walk at Hingringham Hall, Norfolk.

A great number of nut trees appear in the lists. In 1796 208 were ordered (173 filberts, 23 almonds, 5 cobnuts, 7 yellow chestnuts), and these must have been for planting a nut walk. A nut walk provided another harvest for winter storage but was also prized as a cool, dark tunnel to walk in from July to September. [Fig. 18] There are other entries that are slightly puzzling: in 1785 12 standard almond orchard trees, and 18 'double' orchard trees (8 peaches, 6 cherries and 4 almonds) were listed. 'Double' trees (i.e., double flowered) are described by Phillip Miller as being for ornamental purposes

> When the new Orchard was planted on Monday Dec 16th 1799, were planted also, about the Premises and in the aforesaid Orchard, Forty-seven Walnut trees, a Present to George Purefoy Jervoise Esq of Herriard House, Hants, from Daniel Hobson, Esq of Somerley House, near Ringwood, Hants.

Apart from providing nuts for the table, a plantation of walnut was a serious investment for the future because of the high price its fine wood would eventually command.

Vegetables for the Kitchen Garden

As with the fruit, the annual vegetable order for seeds and plants to nurseryman John Armstrong increased dramatically in 1796/7. An astonishing range of vegetables was grown: the ordered items read like a list from a contemporary catalogue. [Fig. 19] The full list is at Appendix 3.

There is nothing in the Herriard archives to show how the kitchen garden and greenhouse would have been planted, but we do have clues. Firstly, in Philip Miller's *The Gardeners Kalendar*. Originally published in 1731, this became the gardener's bible, 'directing what works are necessary to be done every month in the Kitchen, Fruit and Pleasure Gardens, and in the Conservatory'. And secondly with the naturalist Gilbert White, working in his garden some 40 years before Herriard's walled garden was built, but only a few miles away at The Wakes in Selborne.

In 1747 White bought a copy of Miller's *The Gardeners Dictionary* and on 7 January 1751 began his own *Garden Kalendar*, recording the growing methods and innovations that he used taking 'whatever opportunity arose to grow the unusual or slightly difficult'.[54] But what were the unusual and slightly difficult? While making a tour to see former college friends in Wiltshire and Devon, he was shown seakale, the seed of which he brought back to Selborne and sowed the following year, 1751.[55] According to the seed merchant Thomas Etty, seed was available by 1753.[56] The earliest known reference to it is in John Evelyn's *Acetaria: A Discourse of Sallets* (1699) tells us that 'there is a Beet growing near the Sea, which is the most delicate of them all.'[57] Evelyn called seakale *capitata marina*; we now know it as *Crambe maritima* and it is a member of the cabbage family. The young shoots of seakale can be forced and blanched and eaten as a delicacy; Gilbert White grew his on a hot bed. In 1797 50 plants were ordered for the new kitchen garden at Herriard. [Fig. 20]

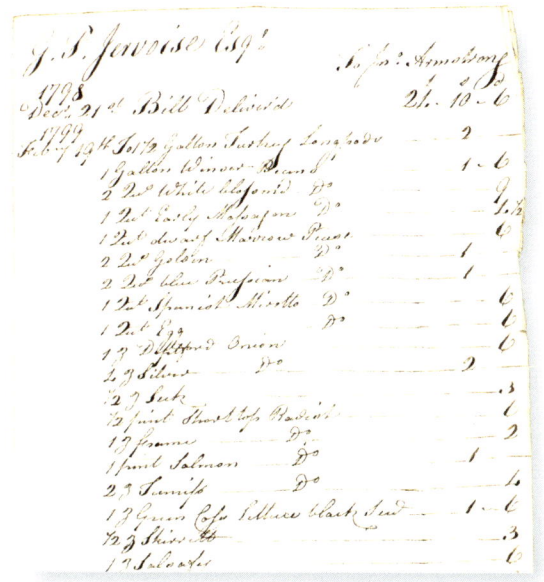

Fig. 19 – A vegetable seed order dated February 19th 1799

31

Fig. 20 – Sea Kale grows wild all along the Solent shore. Traditionally it was forced by piling shingle around new shoots and marking the spot with a stick. When leaves appeared at the top of the shingle pile, the blanched shoots beneath were ready to cut.

We know that the Romans brought crops of Mediterranean origin to Europe, including peas, oats and rye, and that the Arab invaders of Spain introduced rice, sugar cane, sorghum and some citrus fruit. The voyages of Columbus in the 15th century meant the first American crops of maize, tomatoes, chillies and potatoes arrived, also via Spain. The almond and apricot were introduced from Asia in 1548, and the peach in 1562. By the 18th century all food plants that are now of importance in Europe had been introduced, even if not widely taken up.[58] Although the Irish were the first people in Europe to make great use of the potato, it was not widely planted in other parts of the British Isles and didn't become a staple in the diet of the working classes until the late 18th century.[59] It seems that Jane Austen's mother was a skilled grower of potatoes, which in rural Hampshire in the 1760s were still considered an outlandish novelty. She advised a tenant's wife to plant them: the good lady replied: 'No, no, they are very well for you gentry, but they must be terribly costly to rear.'[60] In 1759 Gilbert White raised 3 bushels (about 76kg) of potatoes, some weighing a pound each, from 14 large ones cut into pieces. From this he 'Put by about 30 of the finest as a supply crop for next year'.[61] At Herriard potatoes were ordered in only three years between 1793 and 1799. This may be because part of each crop was kept for sowing the following year, following White's example.

Gilbert White did not have a glasshouse (unlike Herriard), but he made full use of a hot bed, positioned near the stables to take advantage of the fresh manure on which he started seedlings and grew quantities of melons and cucumbers. His *Kalendar* gives detailed information of the construction and the mix of fresh manure and

Fig. 21 – Drawings showing how hot beds, pits and frames were used in the kitchen garden.

33 VEGETABLES FOR THE KITCHEN GARDEN

tanner's bark. It also describes his experiments with allowing air to circulate to prevent the fruit rotting.[62] The use of hot beds vastly helped to prolong the growing season and allowed for a quick succession of planting for many early vegetables: Miller urged the starting of peas and beans every fortnight from February onwards. This was very intensive work: maintaining the temperature of the hot beds required constant attention. Too hot and the plants would scorch; too cold and they would perish; too little air and they would stew and rot. The 1818 plan of the Herriard kitchen garden shows, to one side of the greenhouse and crucially near to the stables, a 'melon ground'. This would have been an area of hot beds and frames to grow melons and cucumbers and to force early vegetables. [Fig. 21]

Miller in his *Kalendar* divides each month into four sections to show what work is to be done in the Kitchen Garden, Fruit Garden, Pleasure Garden and Wilderness, and lastly the Green House and Stove. He also lists, at the end of each section, what plants can be expected to be in flower or fruit that month, and it becomes obvious that the greenhouse was kept for tender flowers, shrubs and exotics – and that it was pretty crowded. We have further evidence of what was grown in Hampshire greenhouses from a sale catalogue of the auction on 22 August 1784 of the house and garden of Hartley Mauditt House, near Selborne.[63] The hothouse contained 100 fruiting pineapples, and the greenhouse mainly flowering plants and shrubs, including potted orange and lemon trees. We have found no evidence for citrus fruit being grown in the new kitchen garden at Herriard, although we know from a letter from Richard Fry to Jervoise in 1794 that there was a previous greenhouse that housed them, possibly the greenhouse noted earlier on the George London plans or a later structure. 'Eades was here yesterday with Mr Armstrong's man & budded the Orange Trees in the Green House & have cut another Mellon [*sic*] which I have sent with Other fruit'.[64]

The kitchen garden at Herriard cannot have accommodated all the vegetable seeds and plants that were ordered. Miller tells us that brassicas must be set two feet apart and that one gallon of broad beans is about 1,600 seeds and would make 7 by 60ft rows. Most of the hardy and winter-hardy vegetables would have been grown as field crops outside the walls. Some orders are puzzling, for example those in 1797 for 2,725 asparagus plants, which conjures up an absolutely enormous asparagus bed. At the standard planting distance of 12 inches and row spacing of 18 inches, the bed would have measured some 27 x 17 yards. Possibly some of the crowns were used in the flower beds as ferns, but asparagus was forced in order to produce spears for the table from January onwards. As asparagus was a fashionable vegetable, it is also possible that some of the crop was grown for sale. Gilbert White was personally involved in all aspects of work in his garden, but Herriard was on an altogether grander scale. When the new kitchen garden was built, George Purefoy Jervoise was a young bachelor: it would be interesting to know who were the recipients of all this produce. Did he entertain lavishly or was it all for show and status?

Tree planting and hedge laying

It is clear from the archive that Jervoise embarked on a substantial programme of tree planting and hedge laying on the Herriard estate, some of which seems to conform to principles that Repton later wrote down in his books. Between 1794 and 1800 Jervoise planted almost 15,000 native and naturalized deciduous trees and 400 pines and firs. Of the 15,000 native trees, 11,600 were ash planted in one tranche in 1794 at cost of between two shillings and three shillings per hundred, depending on size. Other plantings in smaller numbers included beech, birch, elms, hornbeams, horse chestnuts, oaks, planes, poplars, sycamores – probably for ornamenting the park. Similarly the non-native firs and pines were prized for adding variety to the limited range of native evergreens. Brown had mixed firs and pines into park perimeter belts to create varied light and shade effects, an idea Repton continued. The 'Balm O'Gilead', a balsam fir native to northern North America and Canada, was popular, as were Cypress ,'Scotch Firrs' [sic], Weymouth pines and Red Cedar. [Fig. 22] However, Repton was not a great fan of the pines and firs. He advised one client to plant only beech and subsequently scolded him for proposing to add a few cedars, pineasters and silver firs to the mix: 'I have frequently observed that, in planting a tree, few persons consider the future growth or shape of different kinds. Thus the beech and the

Fig. 22 – A veteran tree in Herriard Park.

ash will admit of a view under their branches; while the fir tribe and conic-shaped trees will not.'[65]

In the winter of 1798 almost 3,000 hollies were ordered, and a further 1,000 in 1800. This quantity of hollies suggests their use was to protect young trees from being browsed by animals. Fast-growing birch was also used to protect young plantations, being taken out as slower-growing trees matured. Repton prescribed:

> Let the staple of our plantations be oak and Spanish chestnut, let the copse be hornbeam or hazel; and let the trees used as nurses be birch; but, above all, let there be at least five or six thorns and hollies for every tree that is planted; these will grow up with the trees, perhaps choke and destroy some, but they will rear many, and in a few years will become an impenetrable thicket, as a cover for game, and a harbour for deer.[66]

Fig. 23 – Possibly a multi-stemmed tree planting near the old kitchen garden at Herriard.

All through this period hedge-laying was going on in the estate on an industrial scale. Cuttings, usually of *Crataegus oxyacantha* (common white thorn) were called 'quicksets' (quick as in alive, not fast). Between the winters of 1795 and 1798 over 20,000 were planted. An entry in November 1797 records '144 rod of Quicksets, 1 man 1 day planting 1000 quicksets'. 144 rod converts to 725 metres: if the 1,000 quicksets were the 144 rod's worth, then the planting interval would be just over 70 centimetres, which sounds about right to grow a dense hedge. It was back-breaking work.

Of great interest in the archive is the huge range of ornamental or specimen trees ordered in ones or twos, a total of 460 over the same period. Some names in the order lists were unfamiliar and difficult to identify: the complete list with identification notes is at Appendix 4. The range and diversity of these trees would have created a rich tapestry of colour and texture throughout the year. In *An Inquiry into the Changes of Taste in Landscape Gardening* (1806), Repton expounded on the many contrasts that could be created by imaginative planting. Here is a sample: 'The next contrast ... is that of light and dark ... of a variety in colouring observable in nature and well worth cultivating in the art of gardening.'[67]

Repton had strong views about how trees should be planted. He was scathing about those gardeners who could not envisage any method other than planting in rows at regular intervals, like turnips, he said. In forests, 'we most admire those double trees, or thick clusters, whose stems seem to rise from the same root'.[68] Therefore, to produce this effect he specified that two or more trees should sometimes be planted in the same hole, cutting their roots to bring them closer together. At Herriard today there are a few surviving examples of this method of tree planting. [Fig. 23]

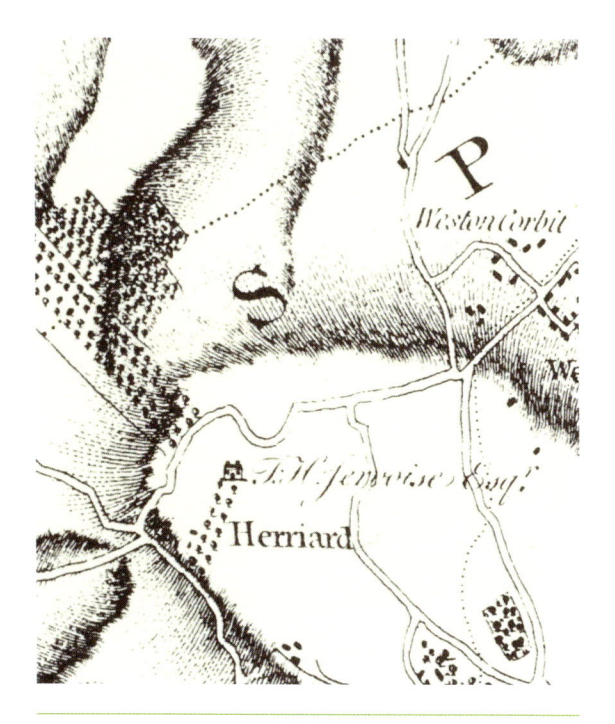

Fig. 24 – The double avenue in Herriard Park extends NW. Detail from Thomas Milne's one-inch map of Hampshire, 1791.

Fig. 25 – The Avenue, on axis with the house; the octagonal kitched garden lies SW of the house.

In all his publications Repton mentions Herriard only once, in a passage about how to 'break' an old avenue by creating openings to new vistas. However, he wrote:

> An avenue of firs is the most obstinate to break … and, therefore, in the stupendous double row of large silver firs, which the false taste of the last century has planted at Herriard's house, I have advised the destruction of one half, leaving the other as a magnificent specimen of the ancient style of gardening.[69]

The avenue first appears on Milne's map of 1791, but it probably dated from the previous century, when long avenues projecting into the landscape served to emphasize the grandeur and status of the houses that they heralded. [Fig. 24] From succeeding maps it looks as though Repton's advice was followed and part at least (if not half) of the avenue was felled. Richard Fry in a letter to Jervoise dated January 1795 reported:

> I have imployed [sic] 3 men cutting the Firs in … the Avenue. The Firs … brought to the Timber yard but many of them are unsound – there is one single row cutt [sic] in the Avenue but we are obliged to stop cutting & faggot up the Lop of those cut before we can throw any more without great Damage.[70]

Repton's acknowledgement of the magnificence of the avenue may have chimed with Jervoise's wish to preserve tangible evidence of Herriard's history and his inheritance. The truncated avenue survives, replanted several times with different species but on the original footprint. [Fig. 25]

Plantations and Shrubberies

In his bills, Repton refers to the 'Plantations' at Herriard, the usual word at that time to describe a planting of trees mixed with ornamental and flowering shrubs. By the time the 1818 plan was made, the fashionable word was 'shrubberies', a word more familiar to us. Existing or planted native trees, thorns and evergreens could be transformed into picturesque and fashionable shrubberies with the addition of ornamental and fragrant shrubs such as syringa. Repton used the terms interchangeably: 'I propose to conduct walks through shrubberies, plantations and small sequestered lawns, sometimes winding into rich internal scenery.'[71]

The idea was not new: 'Capability' Brown had planted shrubberies despite the popular image of mansions set in sweeping green turf set with specimen trees as the archetypal Brown landscape. A shrubbery near enough to the house for convenience with a dry gravel walk winding through it was a valuable addition to the recreational value of the garden.

Shrubberies abound in Jane Austen's novels as places to walk in fine weather, for private conversation, as a setting for a marriage proposal (as in *Emma*). In several of her novels she reveals her knowledge of fashionable garden design – and of Repton. In *Mansfield Park* Fanny Price enthuses about the shrubbery of the parsonage:

> This is very pretty … every time I come into this shrubbery I am more struck with its growth and beauty. Three years ago this was nothing but a rough hedgerow along the upper side of the field … and now it is converted into a walk, and it would be difficult to say whether most valuable as a convenience or an ornament.[72]

The 1818 plan (page 22) shows how Repton achieved the effect he desired. From the mansion a meandering path (more interesting in Repton's eyes than a straight one) approaches the kitchen garden and then divides to circumnavigate the walls. But the walls will be glimpsed only occasionally through a screening of trees and shrubs. Although Repton considered the kitchen garden should be close enough to the house to offer a sheltered walk and – of course – close to the stables so that manure was at hand, it should be screened from view. Between the screening and the walls are the 'slip gardens', accessed from a utilitarian path. The 'slips' were an 18th-century idea to take advantage of the outer sides of kitchen garden walls to grow hardy fruits and vegetables needing less shelter. If more space for vegetables were not needed, the slip would be planted with ornamental shrubs and hardy fruit trees. At Herriard there are old apple trees in the slips, which are not now cultivated.

Fig. 26 – This sketch plan is inscribed on the reverse 'Proposed Alterations for a Pleasure Garden and Orchard at Herriard, introducing thereby a Footpath from the House to the New Stables by John Armstrong of North Warnborough, Nurseryman' and dated September 1st 1799.

The 1818 plan, drawn 15 years after Repton produced his working instructions, shows that his plans were probably implemented. However, there is an earlier plan, drawn in 1799 by nurseryman John Armstrong, showing just the north-east quadrant of the kitchen garden and labelled as 'Proposed Alterations'.[73] [Fig. 26]

In the absence of an earlier plan, it is difficult to determine what the proposed changes were. An orchard is shown, which must have contained many of the fruit trees ordered from 1796, but by 1818 it had gone. However, the area of most interest lies to the south-west of the orchard: an enclosed, turfed area containing one large island bed and several smaller ones. This is another link to Repton. This was called 'forest lawn' planting, a picturesque way of imitating forest glades, popularized as a garden style by several writers in the mid-18th century and most famously implemented in a garden created for Lord Harcourt at Nuneham Courtenay, in Oxfordshire, in 1785. [Fig. 27] Neat, kidney-

PLANTATIONS AND SHRUBBERIES

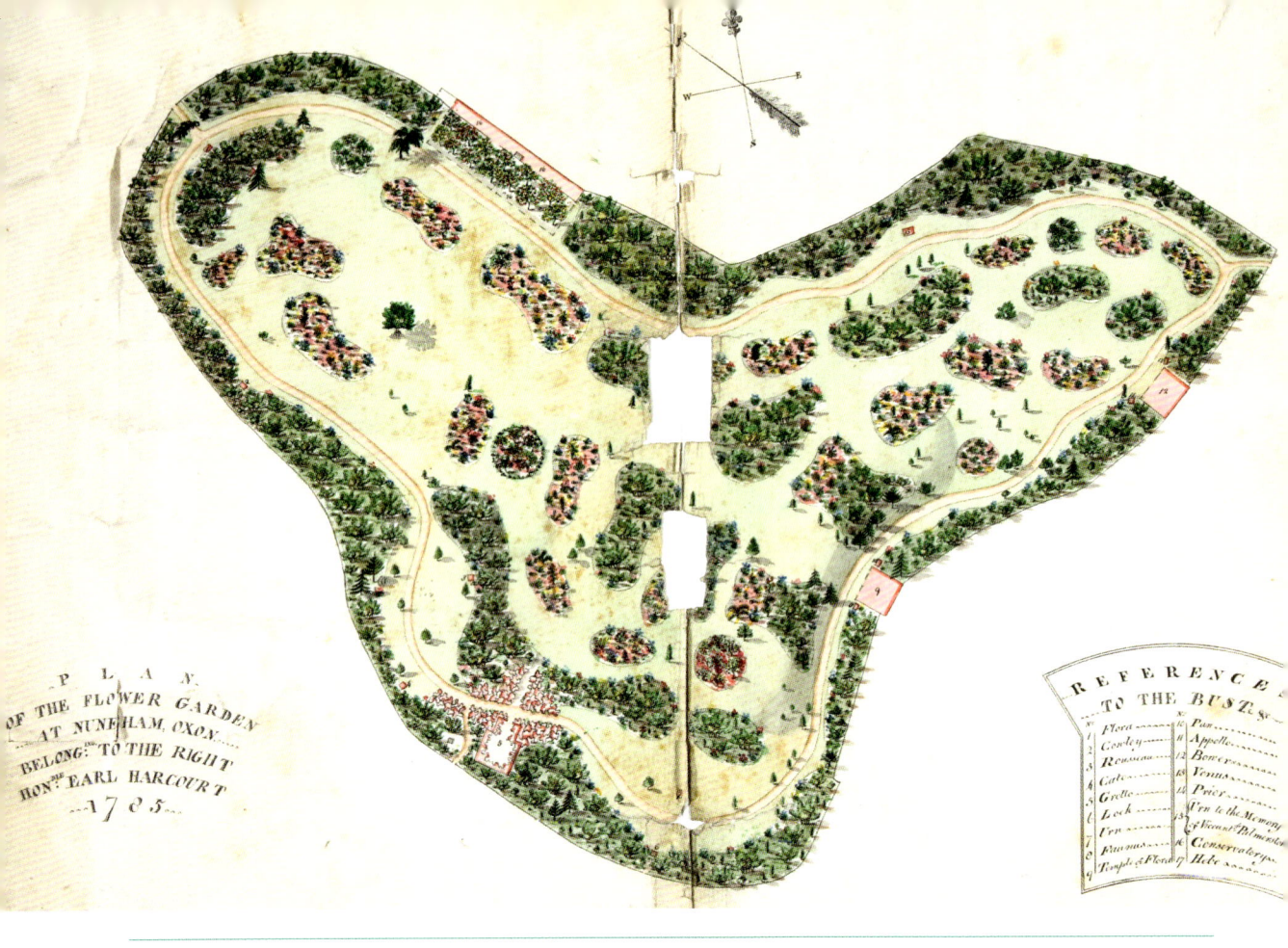

Fig. 27 – Plan of the flower garden at Nuneham Courtenay, Oxfordshire, 1785.

shaped flower beds stud the lawn and winding walks are enclosed by forest shrubbery. Repton visited Nuneham in 1792, and was personally escorted round this garden by Lord Harcourt, who had written a guidebook, which told the visitor how to view the garden with 'poet's feeling and painter's eye'.[74] This would most certainly have resonated with Repton and he sketched the garden. Almost immediately he proposed an 'irregular modern flower garden' for Cobham, in Kent, where he was then working. So these ideas would have been in the front of his mind when he came to draft the plans for Herriard the following year, and the plan of 1799 probably shows that his design (or something like it) was implemented.

From the design of the pleasure gardens around the mansion we can now turn to what the archive tells us was being planted there, which at least in part followed Repton's advice.

In his Red Book for Langley Park in Kent in 1790, he specified: 'House framed by two masses of evergreens, Cedars, Bird cherry, Cypresses etc., with Portugal Laurel and Arbutus in front.'[75] Not a planting scheme to set a gardener's pulse racing and really Repton was not much of a plantsman.[76] He went on to state that a major function of plantations in both park and pleasure ground was to screen kitchen gardens, stables and what he called 'alien property'. But also, because the whole extent of the property could not be seen at once, the grounds would seem more extensive than they were. At Herriard, Portugal and Common laurel and evergreens of all sorts, especially *Phillyrea* (mock privet), were the workhorses of the screening planting and were ordered in large quantities. But there is more variety in the purchasing, which suggests that Jervoise and Armstrong were ambitious plantsmen. The shrub orders are summarized in Appendix 4.

Roses appear frequently in the order lists, some of them very old varieties. They were all (with one exception) what we now call 'old roses': they flower only once, in June. The first China roses arrived from 1792, but it was not until they were hybridized with European roses that the first reliably repeat-flowering roses were bred. Moss roses were clearly a favourite: 57 were bought between 1794 and 1799, which suggests a buyer with an eye for novelty. Moss roses are *Centifolias* that have developed moss-like growth on their sepals (the result of a sport). [Fig. 28] The origin is unknown and the earliest mention in England was 1724, when it was listed in the catalogue of Robert Furber, owner of one of the famous Kensington nurseries. The majority of moss roses were bred over a short period of time in the mid-19th century: they appealed to Victorian romanticism. Therefore the moss roses ordered for Herriard would have been of one kind only and certainly ordered from a specialist nursery. The full list is at Appendix 5.

A gardening principle of the time to which Repton adhered was to exclude all view of fences by replacing them with 'sunk fences' or ha-ha's. However, he also wrote:

> There are a certain class of flowering plants which require support, and these should be amply provided for in all ornamental gardens. The open trellis-fence, and the hoops on poles, over which creeping and climbing plants are graceful spread, give a richness to garden scenery that no painting can adequately represent.[77]

So at Herriard fragrant climbers and twiners were ordered every year: honeysuckles of several kinds; white 'jessamine' (jasmine); 'Trumpet flower' *(Bignonia capreolata)* and 'Sweet Clematis'. It is likely that this was the autumn-flowering *Clematis paniculata*. In 1798 one specimen of 'Cape Jessamine' was bought, but this was *Gardenia jasminoides,* an evergreen flowering plant of the coffee family, originating in Asia. It was introduced to English gardens in the mid-18th century and would have needed greenhouse protection. Its flowers resemble jasmine, and its common name derives from the belief that it originated from the Cape of Good Hope, from where it was probably introduced.

Lists tell us the range and diversity of the planting but not how and in what combinations plants were used: that sort of information occurs more rarely. So it is unusual and remarkable that the archive contains planting lists dated 1795 for nine specific locations around the house and offices.

Rosa Provincialis spinosissima
pedunculis muscosis.
Moss Provence Rose

Rosa ex rubro-nigricante flore pleno.
Double Velvet Rose

Rosa sylvestris Austriaca
flore phœnicio.
Austrian Rose

Rosa lutea multiplex.
Double Yellow Rose

Rosa Provincialis major flore pleno ruberrimo.
Red Provence Rosa

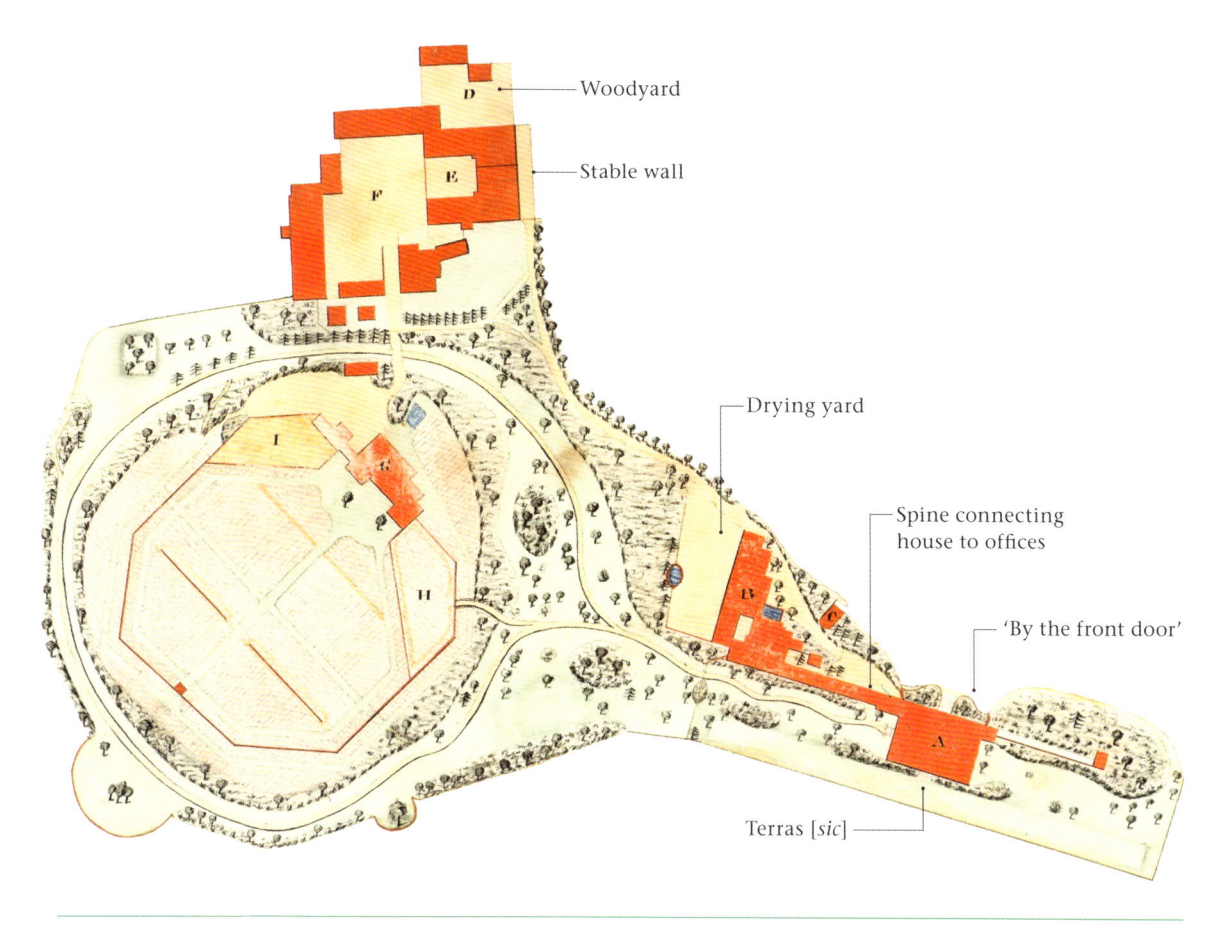

Fig. 29 – The 1818 plan, annotated to indicate planting locations.

The lists below detail the plants that were ordered. NB The spelling used for some plant names differs from today's but has been retained.

'For the drying yard'

Location unknown, but likely to be the area of ground on the NW side of the Offices, which would have contained the laundry.

Trees: 2 double almonds & 2 single almonds.

Shrubs: 1 Azalea; 1 strip'd Box; 1 white Broom; 1 Swedish Juniper; 2 Evergreen Honeysuckles; 2 Phylireas; 1 Arbutus; 1 Persian Lilac; 1 Coccygria; 2 Rhododendron Ponticum; 4 Laurustinus.

Roses: 6 Moss; 1 White Province; 1 Red & Yellow Austrian Rose; 1 double Musk.

Herbaceous: 2 Althea frutex; 1 strip'd Althea; 1 Spirea tomintosa; 2 tomintosa sorbifolia.

'For the Terras [sic] front Row'

The terrace stretched across the garden front of the mansion and was some 300 metres long.

Trees: 2 Ash leav'd Maples; 2 Deciduous Cyprus; 2 Siberian Crabs; 2 sweet scented Crabs; 2 Halisia; 2 Tripple [sic] thorn Accacia; 2 Catalpha's [sic] 2 double Peaches; 2 double Cherries; 2 standard Almonds.

Shrubs: 2 Dahoon Hollies; 6 Portugal laurels; 2 Mespilus; 2 snowy Mespilus; 4 Scarlet Thorns; 1 pear leav'd Thorn. 42 evergreens & flowering shrubs

(continued overleaf)

Fig. 28 (left) – Society of Gardeners, *Catalogus Plantarum*, 1730, plate 18, shows some of the roses ordered for Herriard, including the moss rose (top left).

'For the Terras [sic] back Row'

Trees: 2 double Almonds; 2 single Almonds.

Shrubs: 2 Rhododendrons; 1 Mediterranean Heath; 2 Strip'd Box; 2 Azelea; 1 Swedish Juniper; 2 Austrian Cytissous [sic]; 8 evergreens and flowering shrubs.

Roses: 2 double sweet Briars; 2 Moss; 1 Burgundy; 1 Rose de Mieux.

Herbaceous: 2 white Jasmines; 1 strip'd jasmine [sic]; 2 Evergreen Honeysuckles; 1 strip'd Althea; 1 Green & purple Heath; 1 Erica multiflora.

'By the Front Door'

30 Laurels (large); 5 Laurustinus; 10 Phylireas.

'Wall by the Passage Door'

This location may be on the long spine connecting the house to the offices – a passage between the two.

Trees: 2 double Peaches; 2 Standard Almonds; 2 Siberian Crabs; 2 Mountain Ash; 2 Spanish Chestnuts

Shrubs: 42 Evergreens & flowering shrubs; 2 Portugal Laurels.

'Border on the Left Hand'

Likely still to refer to the area around the offices.

Shrubs: 1 Laurustinus.

Herbaceous: 2 white Jasmines; 1 strip'd jasmine [sic]; 2 Evergreen Honeysuckles; 1 strip'd Althea; 1 Green & purple Heath; 1 Erica multiflora.

'Round the Wall'

Likely still to refer to the area around the offices.

Shrubs: 2 Lilacs; 2 Syringas ; 2 Laburnhams [sic]; 12 Laurels.

'Stable Wall'

Trees: 4 Siberian Crabs; 6 Scotch Firrs [sic]; 4 Scarlet Oaks; 6 Planes; 4 Poplars; 6 Sycamores; 6 Limes; 6 Hornbeams; 6 Beech; 6 Mountain Ash; 4 Bladder nuts; 4 Sumachs; 4 Accacia.

Shrubs: 10 Laurels; 12 Lilacs; 2 Syringas; 4 Laburnhams [sic]; 6 Guilder Roses; 6 Virginian Guilder Roses; 4 Scarlet Thorns; 4 double Thorns; 2 Privets; 2 Euonymus.

'Woodyard'

Trees: 10 Scotch Firrs [sic]; 10 Sycamores; 10 Limes; 10 Hornbeams (large); 38 Beech; 2 Horse Chestnuts; 4 Red Cedars; 2 standard Almonds; 3 Siberian Crabs.

Shrubs: 2 Phylireas; 13 Laurustinus (small); 6 Rhododendrons; 14 strip'd Box; 9 Pyracanthus; 8 strip'd Hollies; 4 Port. Laurels; 2 Candleberry Myrtles; 3 Oleasters; 3 Groundsell trees; 77 Evergreens & Flowering Shrubs.

Roses: 2 Moss

Herbaceous: 100 plants (*not specified*).

These plantings are for the outside walls of the 'alien property', screening them from view but the scale and variety of the planting is quite astonishing. The evergreen planting is ornamented with double-flowered fruit trees, sweet-scented Crabs, Sweet Briars, Jasmines, Roses, Honeysuckles, Lilacs, Syringas – and *Rhododendron ponticum*!

The planting for the terrace, with for instance most of the trees being in the front row, is puzzling when we compare it to our modern idea of planting a border with taller and larger plants at the back, smaller plants at the front.

This was also the formula in the 18th century, as per published diagrams of how to plant five or six gradations of trees and shrubs. However, other priorities could and did amend these rules. As the century progressed, the desire to display choice plants became an increasingly important factor in the composition of shrubberies. A certain tree or plant might deserve a conspicuous place for any combination of its attributes: beautiful foliage, flowers, fragrance, novelty or scarcity. This 'distinction of conspicuousness' could be very important to an owner wishing to display his taste, knowledge and wealth.[78]

Small flowering and ornamental plants

The archive records the quantities of flower seeds, bulbs, herbaceous perennials and the exotic plants needing special care and protection bought between 1794 and 1800: the summary is set out in Appendix 6.

Small flowering plants do not comprise a large proportion of plant orders, yet they give us important insights into the botanical and horticultural developments of the age, as well as the aspirations and interests of George Purefoy Jervoise.[79] Annual flowers were used to give colour and scent to both garden and house, and were usually bought in bulk; for example in 1799 '30 sorts of annual flower seeds' were ordered at a cost of 7s 6d. Some would be for the new walled garden, and some for the pleasure garden and shrubberies; 'Seeds (Flower) for Pleasure Garden & Shrubberies – £1: 1: 3d' appears in a bill of 1798. It is interesting to note that from 1797 onwards, with the construction of the walled garden and work on the surrounding area, annual flower seed orders triple in cost. Only rocket larkspur, sweet peas and mignonette are specified in the seed orders, the former being a popular cut flower, and the latter two grown particularly for their scent. *The Botanical Magazine* in 1790 notes of mignonette that 'The luxury of the pleasure-garden is greatly heightened by the delightful odour which this plant diffuses; and as it is most readily cultivated in pots, its fragrance may be conveyed to the

Fig. 30 – Erica cerinthoides, vol. 7, plate 220. William Curtis, *The Botanical Magazine; or, Flower-Garden Displayed* (London, 1795).

parlour of the recluse, or the chamber of the valetudinarian.'[80]

The bulbs ordered in 1798 and 1800, although far fewer in number than the annual flowers, were more expensive, with individual bulbs often costing 6d or 9d each. They were probably for planting in the pleasure garden or shrubberies as suitable subjects for admiration. Miller suggests that bulbs such as tulips, jonquils, hyacinths and narcissi should be planted in the ground by the end of October.[81] Alternatively, they may be put 'upon glasses filled with water, for to flower in rooms early in the spring' – possibly a preferred option for choice specimens.[82]

With the development of double-flowered hyacinths by the Dutch grower Peter Voorhelm in the early 18th century, hyacinths soon overtook tulips in popularity, though fortunately the craze did not attain the dizzy heights of the tulip mania of the previous century. Between 1794 and 1800 Jervoise ordered only 6 tulips, albeit of the van Thol variety, one of the best-known and early-flowering tulips, at 6d each. During the same period 107 hyacinths were bought. It is not clear whether he was ordering double varieties, though in the 1800 order the distinction is made between 12 Hyacinths (1s 0d each) and 2 single Hyacinths (9d each). It is possible, even likely, that after 1798 Mrs Jervoise had a hand in deciding what was bought – hyacinths to force indoors would be an attractive addition to the décor.

To fill the new beds and borders, 500 unnamed herbaceous perennials were ordered between 1795 and 1799. Pinks (*Dianthus* spp.) seem to

Fig. 31 – Pelargonium tricolor, vol. 7, plate 240. William Curtis, *The Botanical Magazine; or, Flower-Garden Displayed* (London, 1795).

have been a particular favourite, being ordered every year in 1796–1799. Though pinks were growing in English gardens by the 16th century, it was only in the latter half of the 18th century that they became a focus for improvement and joined the elite group of 'florists' flowers'.[83] Jervoise's order for '12 Pinks – the best' for 4s 0d in 1799 suggests that he may have received some of these newer varieties. His order for '2 Indian Pinks in Pots' refers to *Dianthus chinensis*, introduced in 1790. According to

Fig. 32 – Metrosideros citrina (bottle brush), vol. 8, plate 260. William Curtis, *The Botanical Magazine; or, Flower-Garden Displayed* (London, 1795).

Curtis, although 'it cannot boast the agreeable scent of many of its congeners, it eclipses most of them in the brilliancy of its colours; there are few flowers indeed which can boast that richness and variety found among the most improved varieties of this species.'[84]

In addition to buying bulk quantities, Jervoise was clearly pursuing an interest in the new plants arriving in Britain from around the globe, ordering single specimens of named varieties at considerable expense. Many of these would require protection in the winter months, if not year-round, and Repton noted that changes would be necessary in greenhouse construction.

> There is no ornament of a flower-garden more appropriate than a conservatory, or a green-house, where the flower-garden is not too far from the house ... green-houses of the last century ... were all built at a period when only orange-trees and myrtles, or a very few other green-house plants were introduced, and no light was required in the roof of such buildings ... Since that period, the numerous tribe of geraniums, ericas, and other exotic plants, requiring more light, have caused very material alteration in the construction of the green-house.[85]

With the construction of the greenhouse in the new walled garden, Jervoise was also following the horticultural fashion of his age by filling it with a range of exotics from around the world, including a *Celsia linearis* from Peru; a *Salvia coccinea* (scarlet sage), a tender perennial from the southeast USA; a *Metrosideros citrina* (bottlebrush) from Botany Bay; and many plants from the Cape of Good Hope. The second half of the 18th century was a fabulous time for those with an interest in plants – and the money to indulge their hobby. John Bartram had been sending North American plants and seeds back to his English contact Peter Collinson since the 1730s; James Cook's landing at Botany Bay in 1770 led to the discovery by Joseph Banks of hundreds of new species in the vicinity; and in

SMALL FLOWERING AND ORNAMENTAL PLANTS

1772 on Cook's second expedition to the South Seas, he had on board Francis Masson, a Scottish botanist and gardener sent from Kew (by Banks) to the Cape to hunt for new plants. Masson's success in introducing new varieties to Britain led to a craze for Cape plants, chief among them being geraniums (now pelargoniums) and ericas, and as the century drew to a close, Jervoise seemed to develop a particular fondness for the latter genus.

Today, ericas are associated with rather outdated planting schemes of heathers, rockery plants and dwarf conifers, but our own moorland plants are modest in both size and colour in comparison with those from South Africa. These are often the size of small to medium shrubs, with a profusion of long, tubular flowers in a range of bright colours, often bi-coloured, presenting a brilliance that would light up the greenhouse during the dullest months of the year. William Curtis writes: '... there is scarcely any period of the year in which some of them (African Heaths) may not be found to delight the eye with their blossoms.'[86] The abundance of erica species made available at this time thanks to the efforts of plant collectors, and especially Masson (who is said to have introduced about 86 different species from the Cape),[87] appealed to the collecting instinct of those who were able to buy them through the specialist nurseries. Between 1795 and 1800 Jervoise bought a total of 62 ericas, not all different species, costing £4 16s 0d. About half of these were *Erica carnea* and *E. multiflora*, of European origin and usually treated as hardy plants but if kept in a greenhouse, hot bed or heated frame could be made to flower as early as March.[88]

Most of the Cape ericas cost between two and three shillings each, a not inconsiderable sum when two shillings could buy a day's labour. In 1798 Jervoise ordered *Erica Formosa, E. pyramidalis* and *E. cerinthoides*, each costing five shillings. Curtis's description of the latter species sums up the qualities so desired in this genus – novelty, flamboyance and a long flowering:

> The Erica cerinthoides is one of the most magnificent and shewy [sic] of the genus, grows wild at the Cape, from whence it was introduced to the royal garden at Kew, by Mr. Masson, in 1774; it is the more valuable, as it flowers during most of the year: its blossoms are found to vary from a deep to a very pale red. It is a hardy green-house plant, and usually propagated by cuttings.[89]

Unfortunately Cape ericas were not easy subjects for cultivation as they required very carefully controlled growing conditions – lime-free soil, good ventilation, a frost-free environment, and exactly the correct amount of water. It is to be hoped that the gardener at Herriard had the skills to keep these precious plants alive and flourishing in our inimical English climate.

Whose hand?

The wealth of information in the Jervoise family archive about the kitchen garden, plantations and pleasure grounds between 1796 and 1800 still leaves us with questions about whose was the guiding hand. We have seen that many of Repton's ideas were implemented, but he was an intermittent presence and his letters show repeated attempts to re-engage with George Purefoy Jervoise.

In the 1790s the French Revolutionary Wars made it incumbent on the gentry to contribute to the defence of the country by joining the Militias and encouraging all their tenants and acquaintances to do likewise. Jervoise joined the North Hampshire Militia as a Captain in January 1794, rising to Major four months later and reaching the rank of Colonel in 1800.[90] Therefore, during the whole period when he was improving Herriard, he was frequently away at camp or on manouevres along the south coast of Hampshire and on the Isle of Wight. Some of his correspondence illuminates the life of officers of the North Hampshire Regiment:

> Dear Jervoise, I was so excessive drunk last night that I have no recollection of what we agreed about crossing the Water [from the Isle of Wight].
>
> (Note from a fellow officer, n.d.)[92]

> We hope that this will find you in good health & good spirits, as we are, after the thorough mawling which Lord Howe has bestowed upon the Men without Breeches. I believe they will hardly pay us a visit this Summer; but if they should venture I make no doubt of their being well entertained on their Arrival.
>
> (Letter from a friend & fellow officer, June 1794)[91]

The Steward at Herriard, Richard Fry, kept his master informed but occasionally there are exasperated letters that show he was not getting much response. In this instance he was having trouble with workmen:

> As I have had little orders from you I cannot contradict them [i.e. the workmen] – in future if you please I would wish to have full orders or none at all then you would know who to blame ... if you pleased to rely on me more it would be more to your advantage as I should look after the workmen more if I had power to Act.[93]

Jervoise commissioned Repton because he wished to enhance the property and his own social standing. However, it is also interesting to note that in the archive there are catalogues for the library at Herriard that list almost every 'garden advice' book then available:

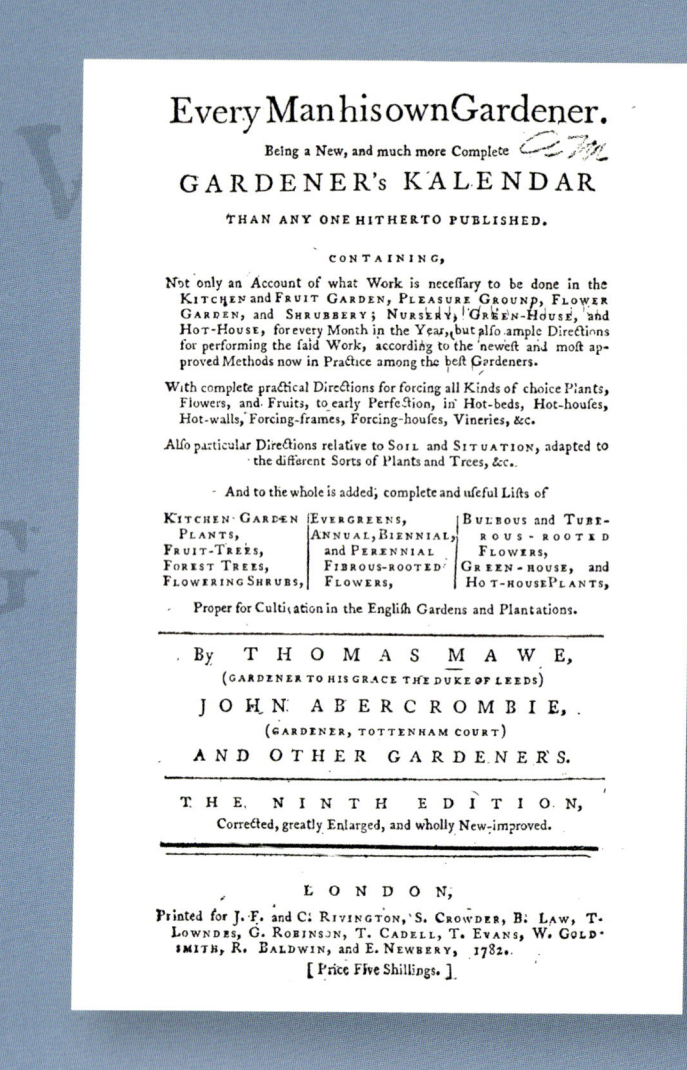

Fig. 33 – The frontispiece of *Every Man his own Gardener* by Thomas Mawe and John Abercrombie, 1782.

several editions of Philip Miller's *The Gardeners Dictionary*; John Evelyn's *The Compleat Gard'ner* and *Sylva*; Batty Langley's *New Principles of Gardening*; John Abercrombie's *Hot House Gardener*; John Kennedy's *Treatise upon Planting, Gardening and the Management of the Hot-House*; James McPhail's *A Treatise on the Culture of the Cucumber*; James Lee's *An Introduction to Botany*; John Abercrombie's *Compleat Wall-Tree Pruner*; Thomas Mawe & John Abercrombie's *Every Man his own Gardener,* and more. Such an extensive collection indicates that Jervoise, and presumably his Steward too, had access to a wealth of information.[94] [Fig. 33] The direction was his, but he would not have had the time to deal with detailed plant orders. Probably that was done by John Armstrong, working with Richard Fry and the named but otherwise unknown 'Gardener' present when the first brick was laid for the new kitchen garden.

John Armstrong, nurseryman (1758–1819)

There were at least two early plant nurseries in Southampton. George Irwin (*fl.* 1743–75) supplied trees for the first plantings of The Avenue there in 1745.[95] Isaac Keen in 1780 supplied trees including London planes to Winchester College for the Fellows' garden.[96] John Armstrong's nursery was in the more rural setting of North Warnborough, near Odiham, but in March 1782 he also sent to Winchester College 24 'Green Holleys' [sic], at a cost of six shillings and 2 'Evergreen Oaks (small)' at three shillings.[97]

The nursery was in existence by 1751 under John Armstrong senior: on 26 October 1751 Gilbert White at The Wakes, in Selborne, paid seven shillings for 'trees & flowering shrubs from N. Warnboro'. The same day he planted 'seven spruce firs from North Warnboro', some flowering shrubs along a walk and a 'Quince tree in the old orchard'.

Armstrong had a number of clients among the Hampshire gentry, including Edward Knight of Chawton House. In 1808 Edward Knight 'Paid Mr. Armstrong a Bill for 2600 withy plants & 12 elms £6-6-0d'. In 1810 he also paid Armstrong for 'Shrubbs delivered at Mrs. Austens £17-19-2d'. These orders were for the cottage in Chawton village that was owned by Knight and had been occupied since July 1809 by his mother, Mrs Austen, and his sisters, Jane and Cassandra. Two or three small enclosures with hedgerows around them were made into a garden, and the hedgerows were transformed into shrubberies by the addition of ornamental shrubs and herbaceous plants.[98] The shrub order is substantial and was almost certainly for ornamenting those hedgerows. This neatly confirms the connection to Jane, who, having experienced the value of a shrubbery, may have based her description of the shubbery in *Mansfield Park* on the one she knew best.

Armstrong held various parcels of nursery land: 7 acres in North Warnborough, a further 8 acres at Dogmersfield, and more. By 1814 his holding totalled 45 acres. We have already observed that he must have sourced some of the huge orders from Herriard from specialist nurseries, of which the largest conglomeration was in west London. Just one piece of direct evidence for this has been found in the archive of Harrison's, a London nursery: '20 August 1806, rec'd of John Armstrong £6-6-0d'.[99] But Armstrong had a substantial amount of ground, and it was the practice at the time for London nurseries, often short of space, to contract out the growing-on of trees and shrubs to country farmers. So perhaps Armstrong was both buying and supplying.

There is also tantalizing proof that Armstrong was a plant breeder in his own right, receiving direct from the Cape of Good Hope seeds of at least one of the exotics then becoming popular.

Fig. 34 – Geranium (i.e. Pelargonium) quinquevulnerum, the geranium raised from seed by John Armstrong in 1796. Henry Adams, The Botanist's Repository, vol. II, plate 114, 1799.

In 1796 he raised *Geranium* (i.e. *Pelargonium*) *quinquevulnerum*. This was recorded by Henry Adams in *The Botanist's Repository*, published in 1799: 'This beautiful species of Geranium was raised by Mr. J. Armstrong, nurseryman of Northwarnborough, Hants, from seed received by him, in 1796, from the Cape of Good Hope.' The entry goes on to record the habit and flowering of the plant: 'it has not, as yet, produced any perfect seeds; although it has flowered abundantly these two years, from May till October.' The drawing for the accompanying plate was made from Armstrong's plant.[100] [Fig. 34]

There is also evidence that Armstrong dispensed horticultural advice: *Directions for the Planting & Management of young Fruit Trees, rec*[d] *from Mr. Armstrong of North Warnborough'*.[101] This document, addressee unknown, is dated November 1772 and includes a sketch intended to illustrate the principles set out. [Fig. 35]

John Armstrong's nursery business ended in November 1814 when it was put up for sale:

> The Old Established and Well Accustomed Nursery and Seed Premises, Late of Mr John Armstrong, containing about 45 Acres of Rich and Productive Nursery, Meadow and Arable Land, The House, Hot House, and Green Houses, Farm House, Barns, Stables, Cottages, Orchards and Gardens, and an Extensive and Commodious Wharf, adjoining the Basingstoke Canal.[102]

Clearly it was a substantial business and it was bought by John Shilling, whose main nursery consisted of 20 acres in Hartley Wintney. In December 1815 the *London Gazette* posted notice of John Armstrong's bankruptcy. He was described as 'of North Warnborough, nurseryman, seedsman, dealer and chapman' (a word meaning merchant or trader).[103] The *Gazette* may have been late in reporting the event, or possibly the sale took place before the bankruptcy was declared. A notice in a London publication suggests that Armstrong had creditors in London, perhaps some of the nurseries that supplied him with stock. It is also likely that, as was common at the time, Armstrong's clients were laggardly in paying their bills.

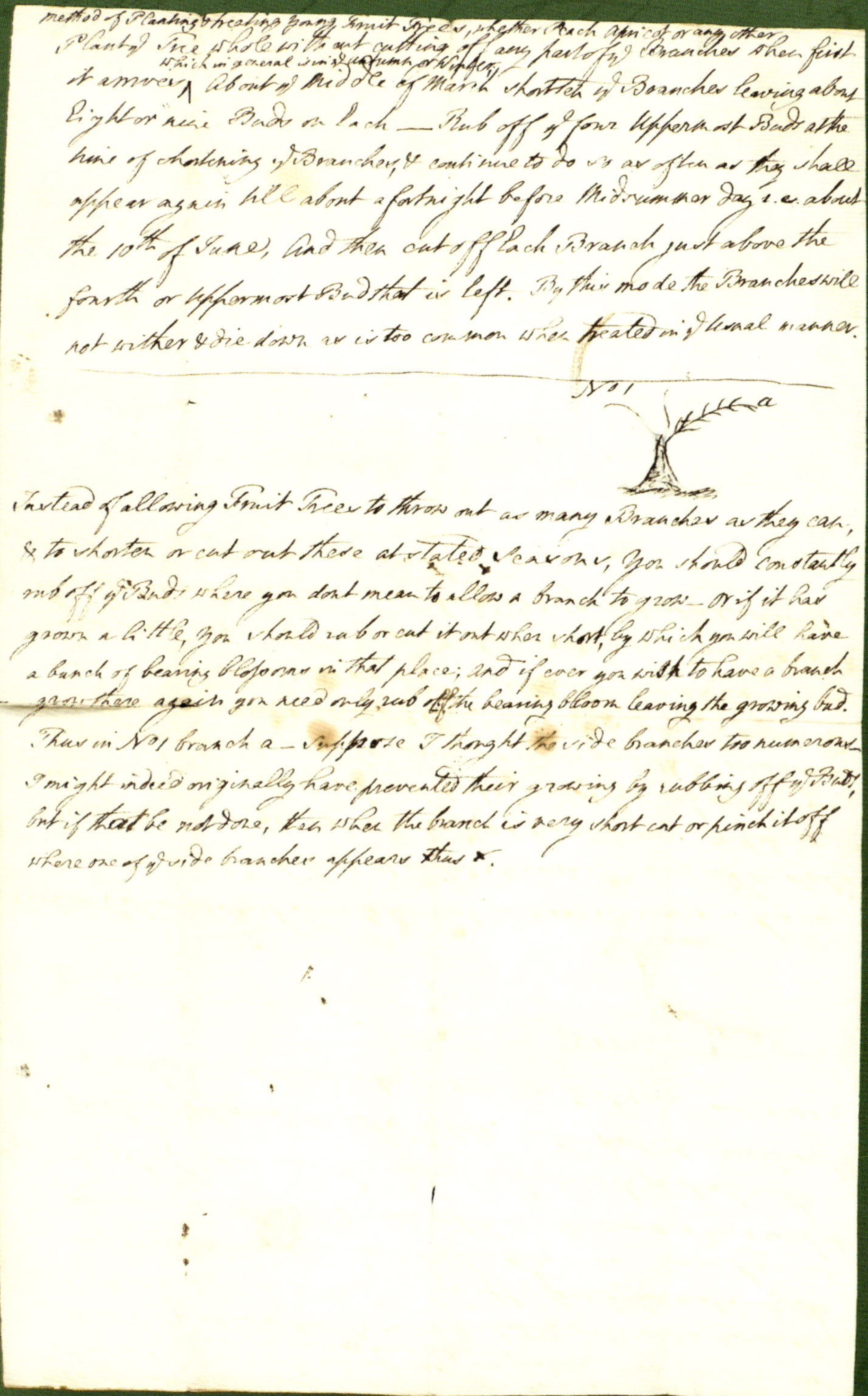

method of Planting & treating young Fruit Trees, whether Peach Apricot or any other Planted Tree should without cutting off any part of y[e] Branches when first it arrives (which in general is middle of fourth of Winter) About y[e] middle of March shorten y[e] Branches leaving about Eight or nine Buds on each — Rub off y[e] four Uppermost Buds at the time of shortening y[e] Branches, & continue to do so as often as they shall appear again till about a fortnight before Midsummer day i.e. about the 10th of June, And then cut off each Branch just above the fourth or uppermost Bud that is left. By this mode the Branches will not wither & die down as is too common when treated in y[e] Usual manner.

Instead of allowing Fruit Trees to throw out as many Branches as they can, & to shorten or cut out these at stated seasons, you should constantly rub off y[e] Buds where you dont mean to allow a branch to grow — Or if it has grown a little, you should rub or cut it out when short, by which you will have a bunch of bearing Blossoms in that place; and if ever you wish to have a branch grow there again you need only rub off the bearing bloom leaving the growing bud. Thus in No 1 branch a — Suppose I thought the side branches too numerous, I might indeed originally have prevented their growing by rubbing off y[e] Buds; but if that be not done, then when the branch is very short cut or pinch it off where one of y[e] side branches appears thus x.

Fig. 35 – John Armstrong's letter with sketch, describing how to prune fruit trees.

JOHN ARMSTRONG, NURSERYMAN (1758–1819)

Postscript

Lavish spending on the mansion and gardens left Jervoise in financial crisis in 1799, as revealed in letters to and from his father that year. His total income between 1792 and 1799 was £32,000, a substantial chunk of which had been borrowed, while his outgoings were £23,000. He wrote to his father:

> 'A prospect with a very melancholy aspect now begins to represent itself before me having only the sum of £240 in my possession the whole of which I expect daily to be called upon to discharge Sums due from me to the Tradesmen in this neighbourhood.'

Moreover, he had not told his wife and was facing the prospect of asking her 'to quit her native Country to seek with me an Asylum where compulsion may invite our removal ... Farewell Society and Friendship'. The letter ends with a postscript: 'Let not, I sincerely implore you, my unhappy sentiments extend beyond your knowledge. For my misery wd. be increased by others being apprized of the calamities my mind daily suffers.'[104]

In 1799 Jervoise had embarked on constructing new stables, and it is this that seems to have precipitated the financial crisis. At the same time, it is clear that the results of the expenditure on house and garden were

Fig. 36 – George Purefoy Jervoise

attracting attention. On 6 July 1799 his wife wrote to him that:

> Just as I was coming by the Front of the New Stables I perceived a Sociable Party coming up the Road from the Church and toward the House ... I learnt ... they had sent here a Note in the Morning ... to request permission to walk in the Gardens. I of course returned with them, shewed them the House &co.'[105]

His father, who had already lent him money, was unable to give him more without 'selling up' and instead advised:

> Honor and Honesty as you observe call on all to pay their debt so they likewise point out to all the propriety of considering before they incur debts whether they have an ability to discharge them. You have resources in your own power & I trust your own good Sense will point out the propriety of making use of them before you apply to any other. In whatever Light you may consider these Sentiments they are I assure dictated for your future good. If they should operate so [?] on you as to induce you to waive for the present the execution of the pursuits you have in View I shall think the time employed in writing them well repaid.[106]

The letters on both sides are long and emotional, but Jervoise did get through this crisis, looked prosperous in later life, as his portrait suggests, and lived to the very ripe age, for the time, of 77. [Fig. 36]

Notes

1 Repton became famous for his morocco-leather bound 'Red Books', designed to show a client how his property could be improved. Drawings and sketches by Repton illustrated improvements using a hinged cut-out device that showed the present scene and, when lifted, the proposed scene. The drawings were set within handwritten text describing the proposed works.

2 Hampshire Record Office (HRO) 44M69/F10/82/1–16 contains all the letters from Humphry Repton to G.P. Jervoise, his client between 1793 and 1801.

3 George Carter, Patrick Goode, Kedrun Laurie, *Humphry Repton Landscape Gardener 1752–1818* (Sainsbury Centre for Visual Arts, 1982), pp.147–65. This was probably Repton's first visit to Stoke Park (Stoke Edith). The client was the Hon. Edward Foley MP, who introduced Nash to Repton.

4 HRO F10/82/2, 6 September 1793

5 Jane Austen, *Mansfield Park* (Penguin Popular Classics, 1994), p.53

6 *Jane Austen's Letters,* ed. Deirdre Le Faye, 4th edn (Oxford University Press, 2011), p.39

7 There are only two fully authenticated Repton commissions in Hampshire, the other being Stratton Park in 1801.

8 J.C. Loudon, *The Landscape Gardening and Landscape Architecture of the late Humphry Repton, Esq: Being his Entire Works on these Subjects* (London, 1840); *Sketches and Hints on Landscape Gardening* (1795), p.29. Note: this Loudon edition of Repton's works is used throughout this paper. For brevity in subsequent endnotes the reference will cite Repton's book title, and the page number will refer to the Loudon edition.

9 Historic England, Herriard Park, List entry number 1000861

10 John James (c.1672–1746), architect, surveyor, and carpenter, was the eldest son of the Revd John James of Hampshire. James was apprenticed (1690–97) to Matthew Banckes, the king's master carpenter. Through Banckes, James came into the orbit of the leading architects of the day, Wren and Hawksmoor. In 1724 he became surveyor to St Paul's Cathedral after the death of Wren and subsequently received several ecclesiastical commissions, including surveyor of repairs at Westminster Abbey from 1736. James designed both ecclesiastical and secular buildings, mainly in London and the southern counties, but few examples of his built work survive. The style he developed from about 1700 was a plain baroque, as seen at Herriard, Hampshire (demolished 1965) and his own country house, Warbrook, in Eversley, Hampshire. Oxford Dictionary of National Biography (online, 2004) https://doi.org/10.1093/ref:odnb/14609 accessed 30 January 2019.

11 George London (d. 1714), nurseryman and garden designer was apprenticed to John Rose, gardener to Charles II. With others he founded the Brompton Park Nursery in west London and from 1697 led it in partnership

with Henry Wise. Wise administered the nursery while London travelled to clients, designing gardens to be planted by the nursery. Brompton Park became the most famous plant nursery in Europe in the early 18th century. London designed gardens for Longleat, Burghley, Chatsworth, New Park, Richmond, Dyrham Park, Wanstead House and many others. Under the patronage of William III he was involved in all the royal gardens, notably at Hampton Court. *Oxford Dictionary of National Biography* https://doi.org/10.1093/re:odnb/37686 accessed 4 December 2018.

12 He added Jervoise to his surname after inheriting Herriard: the legal process cost £164 10s 0d.

13 HRO 44M69/F10/3/2, November 1785

14 Christopher Hussey, 'Herriard Park, Hampshire', *Country Life,* 1 July 1965, pp.18–22

15 HRO 44M69/E19, Miscellaneous notes, including 'List of Fruit Trees planted in two of my new gardens', and a bill for fruit trees from Geo. London & Henry Wise to The Honble Mr. Jervoise, 1703

16 Sally Jeffery, 'John James and George London at Herriard: Architectural Drawings in the Jervoise of Herriard Collection', *Architectural History,* vol.28 (SAHGB Publications Limited, 1985), p.46

17 After 1796 Repton's eldest son, John Adey Repton, an architect, increasingly collaborated with his father on house and garden commissions.

18 Nicola Pink, 'Improving Herriard: George and Eliza Jervoise's Public Image', unpublished dissertation submitted in partial fulfilment of the degree in Eighteenth Century Studies, Faculty of Humanities, University of Southampton, 2013, pp.7–8

19 Throughout this paper, the website https://www.measuringworth.com/calculators/ukcompare/relativevalue was used to calculate the present value of costs and payments, using 'real wealth' and 'real project costs' comparators.

20 The opening sentences of vol.2 of Repton's manuscript *Memoirs*, quoted in Carter, Goode, Laurie, *Humphry Repton Landscape Gardener 1752–1818,* p.5

21 Letter to William Repton, 9 February 1810 in *Huntington Letters,* Huntington Library, San Marino, California

22 HRO 44M69/E14/4/2/23

23 Repton charged 5 guineas a day for visits plus 5 guineas expenses.

24 As business grew, Repton had his children helping to produce the Red Books.

25 Quoted in Carter, Goode, Laurie, *Humphry Repton Landscape Gardener 1752–1818,* pp.19–20

26 William Mason to William Gilpin, 26 December 1794, Bodleian MS Eng misc. d.571 f.224. Quoted in Mavis Batey, 'William Mason, English gardener', *Garden History,* February 1973, p.23

27 The Speaker from 1789 to 1801 was Henry Addington, MP for Devizes. As 1st Viscount Sidmouth he served as Prime Minister 1801–04.

28 Addington owned Woodley, which he sold in 1801. Repton did a Red Book for Woodley and also worked for Addington at White Lodge, Surrey. Quoted in Carter, Goode, Laurie, *Humphry Repton Landscape Gardener 1752–1818,* pp.147–65

29 HRO 44M69/E14/4/2/23, 25 March 1795

30 HRO44M69/E13/4/2/16, 25 March 1795

31 HRO 44M69/E13/4/2/28, Estate Accounts, 1798

32 HRO44M69/E13/4/2/26, Estate Accounts, 1799

33 'Humphry Repton', *Oxford Dictionary of National Biography* https://doi.org/10.1093/re:ondb/23387 accessed 1 December 2018

34 Cited in Laura Mayer, *Humphry Repton* (Shire Library, 2014), p.24

35 HRO 44M69/E13/2/10, December 1799

36 HRO 44M69/E13/4/2/18, *A List of Persons Present at laying of the First Brick of Herriard Garden Walls. March 31st 1796*

37 HRO 44M69/E13/4/2/2, n.d

38 HRO 44M69/E13/4/2/3, n.d, but the entries for labour costs run to 1798

39 HRO 44M69/E13/4/2/28, *Expenses attending the New Kitchen garden walls, Green House, 1796–1800*

40 HRO 44M69/E13/2/10, 8 December 1799

41 Pink, 'Improving Herriard: George and Eliza Jervoise's Public Image', p.5

42 *Ibid.*, p.11

43 Among the achievements of the 3rd Earl of Bute was the establishment from the 1750s of the royal gardens at Kew with and on behalf of Princess Augusta, widow of Frederick Prince of Wales.

44 The other Repton sites were Tyringhame, Buckinghamshire (pre-1794), Grovelands, Middlesex (1793) and Witley Court, Worcestershire (pre-1806). Information courtesy of Susan Campbell

45 Charlotte Phillips & Nora Shane (eds), *John Stuart 3rd Earl of Bute, 1713–92: Botanical and Horticultural Interests and Legacy* (Luton Hoo Estate, 2014), p.38

46 Humphry Repton, *Sketches and Hints on Landscape Gardening* (1795), p.86

47 Humphry Repton, *Fragments on the Theory and Practice of Landscape Gardening* (1816), p.560

48 HRO 44M/69/F10/27/1, letters from Richard Fry to G.P. Jervoise, 24 August and 10 October 1794

49 J.C. Loudon, *An Encyclopaedia of Gardening*, 8 vols, 1838, p.276

50 E.J. Willson, *West London Nursery Gardens* (Fulham and Hammersmith Historical Society, 1982), p.2

51 Philip Miller, *The Gardeners Dictionary*, vol.1, 1754, courtesy of the University of Michigan https://archive.org/details/gardenersdictio03millgoog/page/n307 accessed 22 August 2018

52 Susan Campbell, *A History of Kitchen Gardening* (London, Frances Lincoln, 2005), pp.69–70

53 *Ibid.*, pp.72–3

54 Paul Foster & David Standing, 'Landscape and Labour, Gilbert White's Garden 1751–1793', *Selborne Paper Number Two* (Petworth, Gilbert White's House and the Oates Museum, 2005), p.6

55 *Ibid.*, p.8

56 www.thomasetty.co.uk/seed/vegetables/veg_seed_timeline.pdf accessed 18 September 2018

57 John Evelyn, Acetaria: *A Discourse of Sallets*, 1699 (Brooklyn Botanic Garden, 1937), p.11

58 G.B. Masefield, M. Wallis, S.G. Harrison, B.E. Nicholson, *The Oxford Book of Food Plants* (Oxford University Press, 1969), p.195

59 *Ibid.*, p.176

60 Lucy Worsley, *Jane Austen at Home* (London, Hodder & Stoughton, 2017), p.23

61 Gilbert White, *The Garden Kalendar 1751–71*, entry for 14 November 1759 (facsimile; London, Scholar Press, 1975)

62 *Ibid.*, entries for 23, 24, 25 February 1758

63 Jane Hurst, *Hartley Mauditt House* (Alton, Alton Papers, 2015), pp.42–4

64 HRO 44M/69/E10/27/1. 22 August 1794

65 Humphry Repton, *Fragments on the Theory and Practice of Landscape Gardening* (1816), p.467

66 Humphry Repton, *An Inquiry into the Changes of Taste in Landscape Gardening* (1806), p.451. Birch trees, being fast growing, were commonly used to shelter and protect young, slower-growing trees, usually being taken out when no longer needed.

67 *Ibid.*, p.48

68 *Ibid.*, p.335

69 Humphry Repton, *Sketches and Hints on Landscape Gardening* (1795), p.66

70 HRO 44M69/F10/28/2, 21 January 1795.

71 Humphry Repton, *Sketches and Hints on Landscape Gardening* (1795), p.42

72 Jane Austen, *Mansfield Park* (London, Penguin Books Ltd, 1994), p.210

73 HRO 44M69/P1/72

74 Mavis Batey, 'Poet's Feeling and Painter's Eye: Mason's Flower Garden', *Flowers in the Landscape, Eighteenth Century Flower Gardens and Floriferous Shrubberies* (papers from a seminar held at Hartwell House, Buckinghamshire Gardens Trust, 2006), p.7

75 Notes on Repton's plan for the pleasure ground at Langley Park, cited Carter, Goode, Laurie, *Humphry Repton Landscape Gardener 1752–1818*, pp.48–9

76 David C. Stuart, *Georgian Gardens*, (London, Robert Hale, 1979), p.114

77 Humphry Repton, *Fragments on the Theory and Practice of Landscape Gardening* (1816), p.536

78 Mark Laird, *The Flowering of the Landscape Garden, English Pleasure Grounds 1720–1800* (Philadelphia, University of Pennsylvania Press, 1999), pp.249–53

79 *Ibid.*, pp.249–53

80 William Curtis, *The Botanical Magazine; or, Flower-Garden Displayed* (London, 1790), vol.1, plate 29. Courtesy Missouri Botanical Garden: http://botanicus.org accessed September 201

81 Philip Miller, *The Gardeners Kalendar*, 14th edn (London, 1765), p.320 https://books.google.co.uk accessed August 2018

82 *Ibid.*, p.327

83 Ruth Duthie, *Florists' Flowers and Societies*, (Aylesbury, Shire Publications Ltd, 1988), p.73

84 William Curtis, *The Botanical Magazine; or, Flower-Garden Displayed* (London, 1790), vol.1, plate 25. Courtesy Missouri Botanical Garden: http://botanicus.org accessed online September 2018.

85 Humphry Repton, *Observations on the Theory and Practice of Landscape Gardening* (1803), p.216

86 William Curtis, *The Botanical Magazine; or, Flower-Garden Displayed* (London, 1795), vol.10, plate 342 Courtesy Missouri Botanical Garden: http://botanicus.org accessed online September 2018

87 E.C. Nelson & E.G.H. Oliver, 'Cape heaths in European gardens: the early history of South African Erica species in cultivation, their deliberate hybridization and the orthographic bedlam', *Bothalia*, vol.34, no. 2 (2004), pp.127–40

88 William Curtis, *The Botanical Magazine; or, Flower-Garden Displayed* (London, 1790), vol.1, plate 11. Courtesy Missouri Botanical Garden: http://botanicus.org accessed online September 2018

89 *Ibid.*, (London, 1794), vol.7, plate 220

90 *The Hampshire Militia*, 1757–1894, 1894, HRO shelf ref.H.356.11

91 HRO 44M69/F10/27/1, June 1974

92 HRO 44M69/F10/28/2

93 HRO 44M/69/F10/27/1, 14 August 1794

94 HRO 44M69/M2/1/17, *Catalogue of books in the Library at Herriard House*. John Kennedy ran the Vineyard Nursery in Hammersmith. A famous and well-connected nursery dealing in exotics, he supplied the Empress Josephine with plants and was rumoured to have a passport allowing him the travel between England & France during the Napoleonic Wars.

95 John H. Harvey, *Early Nurserymen* (London and Chichester, Phillimore & Co. Ltd, 1974), p.71

96 *Ibid.*, p.99

97 *Ibid.*, p.100

98 Mavis Batey, *Jane Austen and the English Landscape* (London, Barn Elms Publishing, 1996), p.110

99 London Metropolitan Archive, B/HRS/1, Account Book 1775–1806

100 Henry Adams, *The Botanist's Repository* (1799), vol.II, plate 114

101 HRO 21M57/D60/1, 6 November 1772

102 HRO 10M69/T103, abstracts & titles of Armstrong property 1735–1818

103 *London Gazette*, 5 December 1815

104 HRO 44M69/F9/3/3, 1 November 1799

105 Cited in: Pink, 'Improving Herriard: George and Eliza Jervoise's Public Image', p.11

106 HRO 44M69/F10/1/10, 3 December 1799

Appendices

Appendix 1
Analysis of expenditure relating to construction of the walls of the new Kitchen Garden, 1796   62

Appendix 2
Fruit trees and bushes ordered   64

Appendix 3
Vegetable seed and plants ordered   66

Appendix 4
Trees ordered   70

Appendix 5
Shrubs ordered   82

Appendix 6
Seed, bulb and small flowering/ornamental plant orders   88

Appendix 1

Analysis of expenditure relating to construction of the walls of the new Kitchen Garden, 1796

Materials	Quantity	Price	Cost	Supplier / Source
BRICKS				
Building Bricks	60,976	25s per 1,000	£76 3s 9d	Mr Young of Odiham
Building Bricks	20,000	22s per 1,000	£24 0s 0d	Mr Clarke of Basing
Building Bricks	34,700	25s per 1,000	£43 7s 6d	Mr Clarke of Basing
Building Bricks	29,700	25s per 1,000	£37 2s 6d	Mr Young's Account: Lasham Kiln (Jo^s Turpin)
'Foots' [sic] Assumed to be bricks for footings – which need to be stronger & are more expensive	11,025	30s per 1,000	£16 10s 9d	Mr Young of Odiham
Large Coping Bricks	1,175	5 guineas per 1,000	£6 3s 4½d	Mr Young of Odiham
Old Bricks used in Foundation of the Wall	200,000	1s per 1,000	£10 0s 0d	Cleaned by Thomas Freeborn of Herriard
White Bricks*	2,000	5 guineas per 1,000	£10 10s 0d	Mr Marshall of Basingstoke
White Weather Tiles	1,000	5 guineas per 1,000	£5 5s 0d	Mr Marshall of Basingstoke
		Total	**£229 2s 10½d**	

* [White bricks are produced if there is little iron or other oxides present in the clay. By the end of the 18th century, these were in demand as being closer to the stone colour desired for a classical façade. Although listed under purchases for the 'Kitchen Garden Work', they were possibly used in refurbishment of the house.]

LIME				
Lime, March – November	31 Loads & 26 Bushels	16s 8d per load	£26 7s 6d	Mr Young of Odiham
'Water Lime in June'	92 Bushels	8d per bushel	£3 1s 4d	Mr Young of Odiham
[calculating from this sum, 640 Bushels = 1 Load]	16 Loads & 8 Bushels	6d per bushel	£16 4s 0d	Mr Clarke
'White Lime'	76 Loads & 36 Bushels	16s 8d per load	£64 1s 8d	Jo^s Turpin, Lasham Kiln
'Grey Lime'	27 Loads & 12 Bushels	16s 8d per Load	£36 8s 0d	Jo^s Turpin, Lasham Kiln
		Total	**£146 2s 4d**	

Cost of Carriage	Quantity	Price	Cost	Supplier / Source
BRICKS				
Bricks	35,200	12s per 1,000	£21 2s 5d	Charles Ackland, Basing Brick Kiln
Bricks	15,500	12s per 1,000	£9 6s 0d	Edward Fry, ditto
Bricks	4,000	12s per 1,000	£2 8s 0d	Samuel Clarke, ditto
Bricks	53,550	15s per 1,000	£40 3s 3d	Edward Fry, Odiham Kiln
Bricks	3,750	15s per 1,000	£2 16s 3d	George Kenley, 'brought by my own team', ditto
Large Coping Bricks	1,175	2s per 100	£1 3s 4d	Edward Fry, ditto
White Bricks			15s 0d	Richard Fry, Basing Kiln
'Bricks & Lime'	26½ Loads	5 per Load	£22 15s 0d	Richard Fry, Basing Kiln
		Total	**£111 9s 9d**	
LIME & SAND				
Lime	16¼ Loads	4s per Load	£3 4s 9d	Richard Fry, Basing Kiln
Lime	26½ Loads	5s per Load	£6 12s 6d	Richard Fry, Odiham Kiln
Sand	26½ Loads		£15 0s 0d	Richard Fry
Carriage of Chalk for the Garden'			£7 5s 0d	Richard Fry
Lime	12½ Qrtrs [*quarters*]	12d per Load	6s 0d	Mr Clarke, Lasham Kiln
Lime	12½ Qrtrs	1s 1d per Qrtr	£0 12s 6d	George Kenley, Odiham Kiln
Carriage of Bricks, Lime, Sand etc 'at Sundry times'			£33 0s 9d	
		Total	**£144 0s 6d**	
		Total of these 4 bills	**£631 5s 5½d**	cf Estimate **£587 18s 6d**

Appendix 2

Fruit trees and bushes ordered

Year	Standard fruit trees	Quantity	Dwarf fruit trees	Quantity
1794	Double Almonds – possibly ornamentals	2		
1795	Almonds	12	Apricots Peach	2 1
1796	Peaches Nectarines Cherries) Cherry plums Plums Damsons Apples Pears Figs	10 (3 trained) 7 (2 trained) 7 (2 trained) 8 4 4 12 4 2	Peaches Cherries Plums Nectarines Pears Apricots Apples	31 (7 trained; 15 French) 24 (5 trained) 25 16 (1 Fairchild's; 1 white ditto) 15 9 6
1797	Apples Nectarines	40 1 Roman, trained; 1 white	Apples Pears Plums Nectarines Peaches	19 19 13 Nectarines: 3, 1 white (4) Peaches: 1 Billegarde; 1 Vanguard; 1 French Mignion, trained; 1 early Galande (4)
1798	Double Peach Double Almond	1 1		
1799	Apricots Peach	36 1 ('Montaboon', trained)	Plum Peach	1 1, double 'Swatch' [sic]
1800	Apples Nectarine	4 1 (trained)	Apricots Apples Pears Plum Peach Cherry	8 8 2 1 1 1

Year	Nut trees (standard & dwarf)	Quantity	Soft fruit	Quantity
1796	Filberts Almonds Almonds Cobnuts Yellow Chestnuts	173 23 8 (dwarf) 5 7		
1797	'Fruiting' Almonds	2	Strawberries Raspberries Gooseberries	1,550 339 (86 Cane; 116 White; 111 Antwerp; 25 'nettlestrips'; 1 flowering) 69 (48 Lancashire)
1798				
1799	Almonds	8 dwarf		

A further order list is not dated, but was almost certainly for the new kitchen garden and for planting an orchard (there are no dwarf fruit trees listed)

Year	Standard fruit trees	Quantity	Soft fruit	Quantity
n/d	Peach	2 Orange; 2 Newington; 1 Nutmeg; 2 Admirable Early; 2 Admirable Late	Gooseberries	18 Red Hairy; 4 Green Hairy; 4 Cherry; 4 Damacene
	Nectarine	3 Red Roman; 2 Violet Hastive Early; 3 Newington		
	Apricot	2 Masculine; 2 Roman	Red Currants	18
	Cherry	2 May; 4 Duke; 2 Harrison Heart; 3 Holmes Duke; 4 Morello; 2 Black Heart	White Currants	12
	Plums	4 Green Gage; 2 Blue Gage, Early & Late; Orlene [sic] Orleans; 1 Bonum Magnum		
	Pear	2 Cresson; 1 First Germain; 12 Brown Buree [sic] Beurre; Autumn Burgamot [sic] Bergamot; 2 Swan's Egg; 3 Large Baking; 1 Uvedale's St Germain; 2 Dutch Wardens		
	Apple	4 Golden Pippin; 2 Golden Rennett [sic] Reinette; 4 Nonpareil; 2 Aromatic Pippin; 2 Wheeler's Russett; 2 Broad-Eyed Pippin		

Appendix 3

Vegetable seed and plants ordered

Key nq = no quantity given; curl'd = curled; spt'd = spotted; oz = ounce; lb = pound; pt = pint, qt = quart, 2 pts = 1 qt; 4 qts = 1 gallon; 16oz = 1 pound

Vegetable	1793	1794	1795	1796	1797	1798	1799
Asparagus					2,550 plants	75 2-year-old crown	
Balsam							nq
Beans							
Broad						½ gallon	
Green Garden						1 qt	
Kidney	1st dwarf 1 pt runner	1 pt dwarf ½ pt runner			1 qt runner	1½ pt spt'd 1 pt runner 1 pt dwarf	1pt spt'd 1pt runner
Massagon	1 qt						1 qt
Turkey Longpod							1½ gallons
White Blossom						1 qt	2 gallons
Windsor							1 gallon
Beet	1 oz red ½ oz white			2 oz red	2 oz red		1 oz mixed
Broccoli							
White	1 oz	½ oz	¼ oz 50 plants	¼ oz	¾ oz	½ oz	½ oz
Early purple	1 oz	½ oz	½ oz	¼ oz	¼ oz	½ oz	¼ oz
Late purple	1 oz	½ oz			¼ oz	½ oz	
Other			¼ oz green			½ oz brown	
Brussels Sprout					1 oz	½ oz	½ oz
Cabbage							
Brown			¼ oz				
Butterseu							1 oz
Dutch					1 oz		

Vegetable	1793	1794	1795	1796	1797	1798	1799
Cabbage (cont)							
Early						1 oz	
Green	1 oz						
Hollow	1 oz	½ oz	1 oz	½ oz			½ oz
Milan	½ oz						
Red						½ oz + 25 plants	
Savoy	1 oz						
Sugarloaf		1 oz			1 oz		
York		2 oz	1 oz	3 oz	2 oz	1 oz	2 oz
Cardoon							1 oz
Carrot		4 oz	3½ oz	1 oz	2 oz	1 oz early horn 3 oz orange	1 oz early 2 oz orange
Cauliflower	75 plants	¼ oz	½ oz	¼ oz 50 plants	½ oz	½ oz	¼ oz
Celery	½ oz	½ oz		½ oz		1 oz	1 oz
Corn Salad				2 oz	1 oz		
Cress	1 pt	1 pt				1 pt	
Cucumber	frame	2 sorts Patagonian					Green & White Turkey
Endive		½ oz curl'd	nq		1oz curl'd	½ oz white ½ oz green	
Fennel					Seed & plants		
Garlic	nq	¼ lb					
Gourd					nq		
Leek	1 oz						½ oz
Lettuce							
Brown Dutch		¼ oz				¼ oz	
Coss	½ oz	½ oz white ¼ oz green	½ oz green	½ oz 50 plants	½ oz green	¾ oz green ¼ oz spot'd	1oz green ¼ oz white
Batavia						½ oz	

Vegetable	1793	1794	1795	1796	1797	1798	1799
Marjoram					Sweet		Sweet
Mustard	1 pt	1 pt		1 pt			
Onion	4 oz silver 1 oz James'	2 oz	2 oz silver 1 oz keeping	2 oz silver 1 oz James'	6 oz silver 1 oz James'	3 oz silver 1 oz Deptford 1 oz Welch	4 oz silver 1 oz Deptford 1 oz Welch
Parsley	¼ pt curled	curled nq			2 oz curled	3 oz curled 1 oz H'burg	
Parsnip		1 oz	1 oz	1 oz			2 oz
Peas							
Blue Prussian						3 qt	2 qt
Charlton	1 qt			1 qt			
Early frame	2 qt		1 pt				
Egg					1 oz	1 qt	2 qt
Golden		1 qt	1 qt	1 qt		1 qt	1 qt
Hotspur	1 qt						
Leadman		1 qt dwarf				1 qt dwarf	
Marrow	4 qt dwarf		2 qt green	1 qt dwarf			1 qt dwarf
Spanish Mirotto					1 qt	1 qt	2 qt
unspecified	2 qt	3 qt			3 pt		
Potatoes							
Champion	½ gallon	2 gallons					
Kidney					3 gallons		
Lancashire					5 gallons		
Manly	½ gallon						
Purslane					nq		golden nq
Pumpkin					nq		
Radish							
Early frame	2 oz	1 oz		1 oz	½ pt	1 oz	1 oz
Mixed	½ pt						
Salmon		½ pt	½ pt	½ pt		3 oz	1 pt

Vegetable	1793	1794	1795	1796	1797	1798	1799
Radish (cont)							
Short top		1 oz	2 oz	2 oz		3 oz	½ pt
Turnip	2 oz				2 oz	2 oz	2 oz
Salsify						1 oz	1 oz
Scorzonera						1 oz	½ oz
Sea Kale					50 plants	10 plants	
Shallots		½ lb			½ lb		
Skirret					nq	½ oz	½ oz
Spinach	1 pt	½ pt	½ pt prickly	½ pt	½ pt		
Thyme		10 week	nq			nq	nq
Turnip							
Dutch early		4 oz	2 oz		nq	1 oz	2 oz
Early stone						2 oz	
Rill						2 oz	
Tankard						2 oz	

Appendix 4

Trees ordered

Tree purchases 1794–1800

Note: The purchase of 11,600 Ash in 1794 has been omitted from this chart to avoid skewing the scale.

■ Deciduous woodland   ■ Evergreens   ■ Ornamental/Specimen

1794

Natives/Naturalized: Total 11,942				Evergreens: Total 17		Ornamental/Specimen: Total 44	
Ash	2,500 2s 0d per 100	Larch	25	Balm O'Gilead Firs	2	Acacias	
Ash – large	6,000 2s 6d per 100	Lime	37	Cypress	8	Strip'd Elder	14
Ash – large	3,100 3s 0d per 100	Oaks	20	Scotch Firrs	2	Balsams	4
Beech	55	Plane	40	Silver ditto	2	Lombardy Poplar	5
Birch	35	Poplar	15	Weymouth Pine	2	Mountain Ash	4
Elms	30	Sweet Chestnut	5	Red Cedar	1	Strip'd Sycamore	9
Hornbeam	15	Sycamore	40			Abele	1
Horse Chestnut	25					Deciduous Cypress	1
						Norway Maple	2
						Siberian Crab	2

1795

Natives/Naturalized: Total 426		Evergreens: Total 68		Ornamental/Specimen: Total 105			
Beech	81	Balm O'Gilead Firs	10	Norway Maple	11	Yellow Chestnut	3
Birch	43	Scotch Firrs [sic]	35	Ash-leav'd ditto	4	Tulip trees	2
Elms	37			Strip'd Sycamore	4	Sorbus of sorts	6
Hornbeams	25	Weymouth Pines	11	Strip'd Elms	4	Cut leav'd Alder	4
Horse Chestnut	42	Sweet scented Arbor Vitae	6	Scarlet Chestnut	3		
Larch	26	Red Cedar	6	Canada Poplar	2	Bladder Nut	4
Limes	53			Sweet Scented ditto	2	Sumachs	4
Plane	43			Catalpa	4	Prickl'y Cupp'd Oak	1
Poplar	4			Acacias	4	Mountain Ash	16
Sweet Chestnut/ Spanish Chestnut	19			Deciduous Cypress	2	Siberian Crabs	13
Sycamore	53					Scarlet Oak	8

1796

Natives/Naturalized: Total 964		Evergreens: Total 215		Ornamental /Specimen: Total 215					
Beech *1s 0d each*	82	Balm O'Gilead Firs	25	Alspice	4	Mountain Ash	29	Strip'd Alder	1
Birch	75	Cypress *1s 0d each*	16	Athenian Poplar	3	Paper Birch	2	Strip'd Ash	3
Elms *1s 4d each*	56	Larch *2s 6d each*	74	Betula nana	1	Parsley Leav'd Elder	3	Strip'd Elder	6
Hornbeams	454	Red Cedar *2s 0d each*	17	Canada Poplar	1	Prickl'y Cupp'd Oak	2	Strip'd Sycamores	17
Horse Chestnuts	64	Scotch Firr	21	Carolina Poplars	2	Purple Beech	1	Strip'd Horse Chestnut	1
Limes – large	8	Spruce Firr	26	Catalpa	13	Sartorian Maple	6	Strip'd Sweet Chestnut	1
Limes *1s 0d each*	72	Weymouth Pines	33	China Ash	6	Scarlet Maples	2	Sumach	4
Planes - large	24	White Spruce Firrs *2s 6d each*	11	Cut leav'd Alder	6	Scarlet Chestnut	7	Smoke [*sic*? Snake?] Bark Maple	1
Planes *1s 6d each*	38	Arbor Vitae *8d each*	22	Decid-uous Cypress	2	Scarlet Oaks	10	Tooth Ash Tree	2
Sweet Chestnut	16	China Arbor Vitae	6	Fringe Tree	3	Scotch Elms	10	Tulip Tree	1
Sycamores	75			Live Oak	2	Service	1	Varnish Tree	1
				Liquid Amber	3	Siberian Crabs	16	Weeping Willow	1
				Myrtle Leav'd Sumach	7	Snowdrop Tree	7	Yellow Chestnut	9
				Marsh Elder	5	Sorbus	2		
				Norway Maple	9	Stone Crop Tree	2		

APPENDIX 4

1797

Natives/Naturalized: Total 140		Evergreens: Total 82		Ornamental /Specimen: Total 58			
Beech	14	Balm O'Gilead Firs	7	Cornish Elms	12	Robinia	1
Birch	10	Larch	17	Mountain Ash	17	Alspice	1
Elms	9	Red Cedar	13	Cut leav'd Alder	4	Carolina Poplars	2
Hornbeams	13	Scotch Firr	5	Strip'd bark Ash	4	Nettle Trees	6
Horse Chestnut	8	Weymouth Pines	9	Scarlet Oak	6	Sir Chas. Wager's Maple	2
Limes	60	White Spruce Firr	2	Yellow Chestnuts	4	Strip'd Elder	6
Planes	4	Yew leav'd Firrs	2			Accacia	2
Sweet Chestnut	12	Yew	2			Strip'd Sycamore	6
Sycamores	10	Arbor Vitae	25			Strip'd bark Ash	2

1799

Natives/Naturalized: Total 748		Evergreens: Total 58		Ornamental/Specimen: Total 49	
Ash	600	Larch		Strip'd Chestnut	1
Beech	7	Red Cedar	10	Norway Maples	8
Birch	20	Red Cedars in pots	15	Mountain Ash	4
Elms	63	Weymouth Pine	8	Toxicodendron	13
Hornbeams	4	Yews	4	Strip'd Elder	8
Horse Chestnut	4	Arbor Vitae	6	Cornish Elms	10
Limes	24		12	Strip'd Sycamore	4
Oaks	26		3	Yew leav'd Firrs [probably]	1

1800

Natives/Naturalized: Total 230		Evergreens: Total 123	
Beech *9d*	30	Yew *6d*	45
Beech *1s 0d*	20	Yew *2d*	78
Elm	60		
Hornbeam	20		
Horse chestnut	30		
Oak *1s 0d*	20		
Oak *10d*	10		
Sweet Chestnut	30		
Sycamores	10		

Tree identification notes – alphabetical

Name as given in archive lists	Notes	Botanical name
Abele	White Poplar or Abele. Native Europe & Central Asia. Ornamental	*Populus alba*
Acacia / Robinia	False Acacia or Black Locust. Native eastern & mid-western America. Ornamental	*Robinia pseudoacacia*
Alspice	Carolina Allspice. SE America, introduced *c.*1736	*Calycanthus floridus*
Arbor Vitae	Probably White Cedar or American Arbor-vitae. Eastern N. America, introduced *c.*1534	*Thuja occidentalis*
Arbor Vitae, China	Chinese Cedar or Chinese Arbor-vitae. Native China, Korea, introduced *c.*1690	*Thuja orientalis* (now classed as *Platycladus orientalis*)
Arbor Vitae, Sweet-scented	Crushed leaves smell of apples	*Thuja occidentalis*
Ash-leav'd Maple	aka Box Elder, Marsh Elder. Native east & central N. America. Water loving. Ornamental	*Acer negundo*

Name as given in archive lists	Notes	Botanical name
Balm O'Gilead Fir	Balsam fir. Native Northern N. America & Canada	*Abies balsamea*
Balsams	(Possibly) Balsam Poplar or Tacamahac. Native northern N. America. Ornamental. Balsam smell from winter buds	*Populus balsamifera*
Betula nana	Dwarf Birch. Native Arctic tundra & cool temperate regions	*Betula nana*
Bladder Nut	Ornamental. Some fragrant. Flowers and seeds borne in drooping panicles	Probably *Staphylea trifolia*

Name as given in archive lists	Notes	Botanical name
Canada Poplar	Used for screening. Cloned *c.*1750	Possibly *Populus* x *canadensis*
Catalpa	Indian Bean /Southern Catalpa. Native SE America	*Catalpa bignonioides*
Chestnut, Scarlet	Possibly Red Buckeye with crimson flowers. Southern America, introduced 1711	*Aesculus pavia*

Name as given in archive lists	Notes	Botanical name
Chestnut, Strip'd	Probably a variegated form of *Castanea sativa*, mentioned by Miller	*Castanea sativa* 'Variegata'
Chestnut, Yellow	Possibly Sweet Buckeye with yellow flowers. SE America, introduced 1764	*Aesculus flava*
China Ash	Difficult to identify: *Fraxinus chinensis* not introduced until 1891	*Fraxinus* sp.
Cornish Elms	A variant smooth-leaved Elm. Native to Europe	A variety of *Ulmus minor*
Cut leav'd Alder	There are cut-leaved forms e.g. *Alnus glutinosa* f.*incisa*. Others seem to have been introduced much later	Probably *Alnus glutinosa* f.*incisa*
Cypress, Deciduous	Probably Swamp Cypress or Bald Cypress. Deciduous conifer. Native swamps of SE America	*Taxodium distichum*
Firr, Scotch	Presumably Scots Pine	*Pinus sylvestris*
Firr, White Spruce	Native northern N. America, Canada. Ornamental in northern Europe	*Picea glauca*
Firr, Yew leav'd	Not definitely identified. Miller mentions a 'yew leavd fir' with long hanging cones under Abies, but Abies only have upright cones	Possibly *Picea abies*
Fringe Tree	White Fringetree. Native SE America	*Chionanthus virginicus*
Liquid Amber	Probably Sweet Gum tree, attractive in all seasons, noted autumn colour. Eastern America, introduced 17th century	*Liquidambar styraciflua*
Live Oak	California Live Oak/Encina Evergreen, native California 'Live Oak' often refers to evergreen oaks. Could be e.g. Southern Live Oak California, Mexico, introduced 1739	*Quercus virginiana*
Lombardy poplar	Male clone, propagated early 18th century. Ornamental	*Populus nigra* 'Italica'

Name as given in archive lists	Notes	Botanical name
Maple, Norway	Native to Europe but not Britain. Ornamental for autumn colour	*Acer platanoides*
Maple, Sartorian	Probably 'Tatarian Maple', widespread central & SE Europe and temperate Asia, introduced 1759	*Acer tataricum*
Maple, Sir Chas. Wager's	Admiral Sir Charles Wager (1666–1743) had a garden at Parson's Green, London. Introduced from Pennsylvania in 1725. Grown for its large red flowers	*Acer saccharinum* (Laird) or possibly *Acer rubrum*
Maple, Smoke Bark	Possibly 'Snake-bark'. Eastern USA, introduced c.1755	Possibly *Acer pensylvanicum*
Mountain Ash	Rowan, Mountain Ash. Ornamental	*Sorbus aucuparia*
Myrtle leav'd Sumach	Rhus – but difficult to identify the species	*Rhus* sp.
Nettle Tree	Native S. Europe & SW Asia. Ornamental	*Celtis* sp., e.g. *australis*
Paper Birch	Canoe Birch. Native northern N. America. Ornamental.	*Betula papyrifera*
Parsley leav'd Elder	Mentioned by Miller	Probably *Sambucus nigra* f.*laciniata*
Poplar, Athenian	Mentioned in Miller but no modern reference to it	*Populus graeca*
Poplar, Carolina	Probably *Populus angulata* aka *P. deltoides* 'Carolin'. Origin uncertain, probably N. America. Introduced late 18th century	Probably *Populus angulata*
Prickl'y cupp'd Oak	Possibly Turkey Oak, *Quercus cerris*, introduced from southern Europe in 1735	*Quercus cerris*
Red Cedar	Virginia or Pencil Cedar, introduced from North America in 1664. Western Red Cedar (*Thuja plicata*) not introduced until 1853	*Juniperus virginiana*

Name as given in archive lists	Notes	Botanical name
Scarlet Oak	Native NE N. America. Ornamental for autumn colour, introduced 1691	*Quercus coccinea*
Service	Native southern and eastern Europe, long cultivated in Britain	*Sorbus domestica*
Siberian Crab	Widely distributed throughout Asia, introduced in 1784	*Malus baccata*
Silver Firr	2 bought in 1794 – presumably to fill gaps in the silver fir avenue, pre-Repton	*Abies alba*
Snowdrop Tree	Mountain Snowdrop Tree/ Silver Bell. Native SE America. Ornamental. Probably *Halesia carolina*. Introduced 1756	*Halesia carolina*
Snowy Mespilus	Juneberry or Serviceberry. Ornamental. Naturalized in parts of N Europe and areas of England	Probably *Amelanchier lamarckii*
Stone Crop Tree	Probably *Suaeda fruticosa*, a native maritime shrub with leaves turning bronze purple in autumn. Mentioned by Laird as part of a 1760 plant order for Kedleston	*Suaeda fruticosa*
Strip'd Ash/Strip'd Bark Ash	Identification unclear: strip'd refers to the variegated form: Miller mentions a variegated form of the common ash *Fraxinus excelsior*	*Fraxinus excelsior*, possibly variegated form
Strip'd Elder	A variegated form of the common elder, a native shrub or small tree	*Sambucus nigra*, variegated form
Strip'd Elms	Cultivated varieties of variegated elm were available by the 1760s, according to Miller	*Ulmus* sp., variegated form
Strip'd Sweet Chestnut	See Chestnut, strip'd above	*Castanea sativa* 'Variegata'
Sumachs	Stag's Horn Sumac. Native eastern N. America, first recorded in Britain c.1629. Grown for its brilliant autumn colour and decorative fruits	*Rhus typhina*
Sycamore, Strip'd	Probably a variegated form of *Acer pseudoplatanus*, long naturalized in Britain	*Acer pseudoplatanus*, variegated form

Name as given in archive lists	Notes	Botanical name
Sycamore, Sweet scented	i.e. Sycamore. Difficult to identify exact variety	Probably *Acer pseudoplatanus*
Tooth Ash Tree	Unidentified. Possibly an ash species	
Toxicodendron	'Poison tree'. Flowering genus in the sumac family, related to *Rhus*	*Toxicodendron* sp.
Tulip trees	Native eastern N. America, first recorded in Britain in 1688	*Liriodendron tulipifera*
Varnish Tree	Difficult to identify precisely; possibly a species of *Rhus*, native to Himalaya, Japan and China and often cultivated. Ornamental with large drooping panicles of flowers	Possibly *Rhus verniciflua*
Weymouth Pine	Also White Pine. Native Eastern N. America. Ornamental	*Pinus strobus*

Appendix 5

Shrubs ordered

Herriard Shrubs Orders 1794–1800

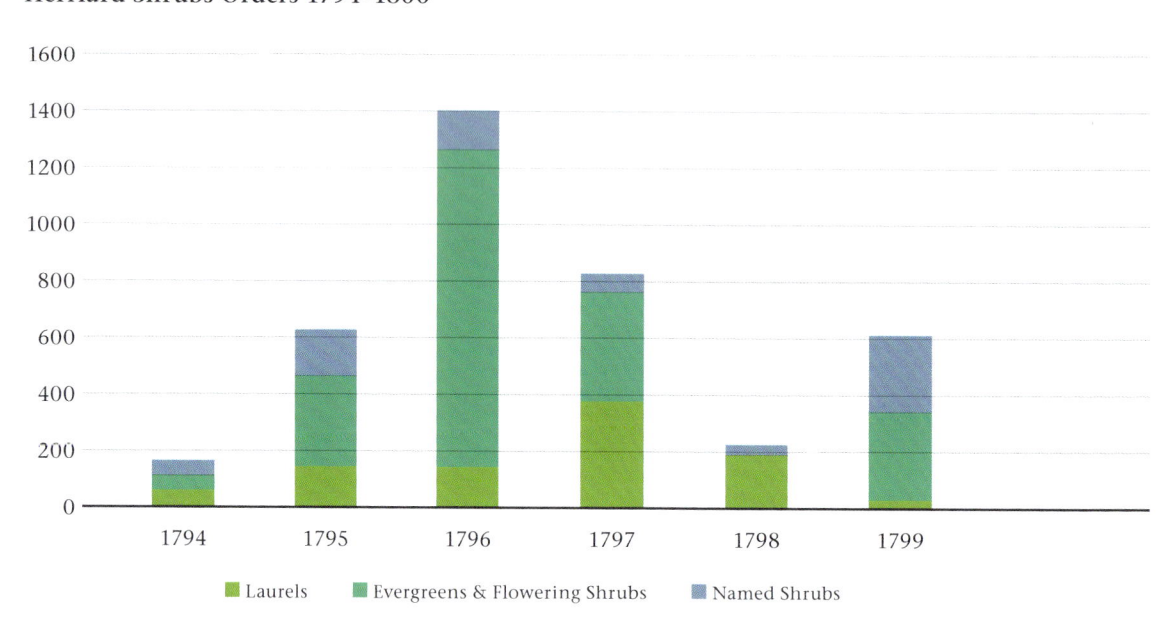

[Bar chart showing shrub orders by year 1794–1799, with three categories: Laurels, Evergreens & Flowering Shrubs, and Named Shrubs]

There is some information in the transcribed archive from which we can interpolate cost estimates for the shrubs purchased 1794–1799.

1794–1799	Price	Quantity	Total
'Laurels' n/s	3d each	633	£7 18s 3d
Portugal Laurels	6d each	132	£3 6s 0d
'Evergreens & Flowering Shrubs' – bulk orders n/s	3d each	2,070	£25 17s 6d
Named shrubs	Prices seem to range from 4d to 9d each: take 6d as mid-point	695	£17 7s 6d
		Total cost	**£54 9s 3d**

Named flowering and evergreen shrubs, ordered in small quantities or as single specimens

The alphabetical lists below are a mixture of common names and the Linnaean nomenclature (not widely known or used at the time). Here, where the list gives the common name, the correct botanical name has been added. Bays, Myrtles, Laurestinus, Cistus would probably have been greenhoused in tubs in winter.

A	*Arbutus unedo* (Strawberry Tree)
	Azalea – probably grown as greenhouse plant
B	Bay (*Laurus nobilis*)
	Box (*Buxus sempervirens*): 'Strip'd' (variegated gold/silver); Broad leav'd
	Broom (*Cytisus*) White; Spanish (*Cytisus multiflorus*); Austrian (*Cytisus austriacus*); Black-rooted (*Cytisus nigricans*)
C	*Ceanothus*
	Coccygria [sic] (*Cotinus coggygria*) Green leaved, introduced c.1656. Other cultivars early 20th century
	Cockspur thorns (*Crataegus prunifolia*)
	Hardy Cistus; *Cistus palmifolia* (palm-leaved); Cistus Leudons [sic], probably *Cistus* ladanifer
	China ArborVitae [sic] *Platycladus orientalis*, formerly *Thuja orientalis*, also included in the tree list, Appendix 4
	Colutea
D	'Dogwood of sorts'
	Daphne cheorium [sic] (*Daphne cneorum*); Mezereon (*Daphne mezereum*)
E	Euonymous [sic]; broad leav'd (*Euonymus latifolius*)
G	*Genista germanica*
	Guilder Rose [sic] Guelder-rose, *Viburnum opulus*; Virginia Guilder Rose [sic]; *Viburnum trilobum*
H	Hollies, strip'd; green Dahoon Hollies (*Ilex cassine*)
	Hydrangea mutabilis (macrophylla)
J	Swedish Juniper (*Juniperus communis* var. *suecica*)
K	'Narrow' Kalmia (*Kalmia angustifolia*); *Kalmia glauca*; (*Kalmia polifolia* – bog laurel)

L	Laurestinus (*Viburnum tinus*)
	Laburnham [*sic*]
M	Mespilus (*Mespilus germanica* – common medlar)
	Snowy [*sic*] Mespilus (*Amelanchier*)
	'Myrtles' Candleberry myrtles (*Morella faya*, formerly *Myrica faya*)
O	Oleaster (*Elaeagnus*)
P	Philireas [*sic*] mock privet, (*Phillyrea*) family Oleaceae (olive)
	'Privets'
	Phyladelphus [*sic*] *diosma*
	'Piriphoca' (*Periploca*), first described by Linnaeus in 1753, primarily a foliage plant
	Pyracanthus
R	Rhododendron (*R. ponticum* – the only one available, introduced 1763)
S	Spiea lavigata [*sic*] Siberian spirea (*Sibiraea laevigata*)
	Syringa vulgaris; *Syringa* x *persica*

Climbers and twiners (totals 1794–1800)

B	Bignonia (*Bignonia capreolata*)	Common names: cross vine, quartervine, trumpet flower	5
C	Clematis 'Double Virgin's Bower'	Common name for clematis	22
	Double purple Clematis	A double-flowered form of *Clematis viticella*, listed by Aiton, vol.2, p.258	
	'Sweet Clematis'	Probably *Clematis flammula*, listed by Aiton, vol.2, p.260	
	Clematis orientalis	*Clematis orientalis* (Asia and Central Europe). Common names: Chinese clematis; Oriental virgins bower; orange peel clematis	
H	'Fly' [*sic*] honeysuckle	*Lonicera xylosteum*, a native of Northern Europe	41
	Dutch honeysuckles	Probably *Lonicera periclymenum* 'Belgica'	
	Evergreen honeysuckles	*Lonicera* x *americana*	
	White honeysuckle	Probably a white variety of *Lonicera periclymenum*	
	Trumpet honeysuckle	*Lonicera sempervirens*	
I	'Five leav'd Ivy'	Virginia Creeper (*Parthenocissus quinquefolia*)	10
J	White jasmine Strip'd jasmine 'Jessamines'	*Jasminum officinale*	41

Roses

The roses available in the late 18th century (bar one) flowered just once annually, in June. The first China roses arrived from 1792 to 1824, but it was not until they were hybridized with European roses that reliably repeat-flowering roses were bred. Many of the roses bought for Herriard were very old varieties and were ordered using old and/or corrupted names.

1794

2 x Proviner [sic] Roses	*Rosa gallica*, or the Rose of Provins, where it appears to be first recorded, similarly the 'White Province rose'. Gallicas are the oldest of garden roses, native to central and southern Europe
4 x Moss Roses*	
17 'Roses & Shrubs of Sorts'	This simply means assorted – whatever the nurseryman has

1795 – These roses all listed as for the 'Drying Yard'

6 x Moss Roses*	
1 x White Province	White *Rosa gallica*
1 x Red & Yellow Austrian Rose	*Rosa foetida*, this was the only yellow rose available at this time, first described in the 16th century. Its common names are Austrian briar; Persian yellow rose; Austrian copper rose; Austrian red (copper) and yellow rose. Native to the foothills of the Caucasus Mountains. Introduced from Persia (via Austria): an important addition to the hybridization of European roses.
1 x Double Musk Rose	
2 x Moss Roses	
1 x Burgundy Rose	A small *Gallica*
1 x Rose de Mieux	A small *Centifolia* rose; a bushy, twiggy shrub with small pink flowers. Said to have originated with a man called Sweet in 1789. *Centifolias* were largely the work of Dutch breeders from early 17th century to early 18th
2 x Moss Roses*	

1796

5 x Moss Roses*	
12 x Moss Roses*	
6 x Burgundy Rose	
2 x Double Musk Rose	

1797

4 x Moss Roses*	
4 x Roses	
1 x 'dark coloured' Rose	

1798

32 'Roses of Sorts'	
12 x Moss Roses*	
4 x Burgundy Roses	

1799

2 x Austrian Roses	
2 x Yellow Roses	
1 x Rosa Semperflorens Pale	Semperflorens ('always blooming'). This is probably the Autumn Damask rose. The Damasks were an early natural hybrid of the Gallica Rose and a wild species *Rosa phoenicia*. The Autumn Damask, a very old rose, is closely related. The only rose to have the ability to repeat flower before the introduction of the China Rose at the end of the 18th century.
2 x Moss Roses*	
10 x Roses	
4 x Moss Roses*	
2 x other roses	

*Moss roses

More Moss roses were ordered than any other type (57 out of 130 roses ordered between 1794 and 1799), which suggests a buyer with an eye to novelty. Moss roses are Centifolias that have developed moss-like growth on their sepals – the result of a sport. The origin is unknown but a rose of this nature was known in southern France around 1700. The earliest mention in England was in 1724, when it was listed in the catalogue of Robert Furber. Furber was the owner of one of the famous Kensington nurseries and part of a circle that included Philip Miller, Thomas Fairchild and Christopher Gray. However, the majority of Moss roses were bred over a short period of time, from 1850 to 1870 (they appealed to Victorian romanticism). Therefore the Moss roses ordered for Herriard would have been of one kind only and almost certainly ordered from a specialist London nursery.

Appendix 6

Seed, bulb and small flowering/ornamental plant orders

Annual flower seeds by year

Year	Seed order	Cost
1794	–	–
1795	annual flower seeds	1s 4d
1796	14 sorts of annual flower seeds	2s 6d
1797	annual flower seeds	7s 6d
1798	annual flower seeds ½ pint +1oz of dwarf Rocket Larkspur ½ pint +1oz of tall Rocket Larkspur 1½ pint of Sweet Peas mixed colours ½ pint Mignonette 'Seeds (Flower) for Pleasure Garden & Shrubberies' Total	7s 6d 6d 6d 9d 6d 1 1s 3d' **£1 11s 0d**
1799	30 sorts of annual flower seeds	7s 6d
1800	36 sorts of annual flower seeds @3d 30 sorts of annual flower seeds @6d Total	9s 4s **13s**
	Total cost	**£3 2s 10d**

Bulbs (none purchased before 1796)

Year	Seed order		Cost
1796	75 Hyacinths		3s 9d
1797	–		–
1798	36 mixed Crocus		1s 6d
	6 Narcissus		3s
	18 Hyacinths		13s 6d
	6 Dutch Jonquils		1s 6d
	6 Van Thol Tulips		3s
	2 Autumn Cyclamen		2s
		Total	**24s 6d**
1799	–		–
1800	12 Hyacinths		12s
	2 single Hyacinths		1s 6d
	6 Narcissus		3s
	6 Double Dutch Jonquils		2s
		Total	**18s 6d**
		Total cost	**£2 8s 9d**

Flowering herbaceous/perennial plants and tender plants – summary

Year	Bulk orders	Plants ordered in small numbers	Total cost
1794	–	–	–
1795	100 herbaceous plants £1 1s 0d	2s 6d	£1 3s 6d
1796	Pinks* 12s	6s	18s 0d
1797	200 perennials £2 2s 0d	10s	
	50 Pinks 12s 6d		£3 4s 6d
1798		£4 7s 9d	£4 7s 9d
1799	200 perennials £2 2s 0d	£3 1s 0d	
	12 Pinks 4s		£5 7s 0d
1800		£1 10s 3d	£1 10s 3d
		Total cost	**£16 9s 0d**

* Pinks are included in the bulk orders, as other named plants were usually ordered in very small numbers.

Flowering herbaceous/perennial plants and tender plants – the detail

Plants ordered in bulk	Cost	Year
100 herbaceous plants for planting in the woodyard	£1 1s 0d	1795
200 perennials various sorts for borders	£2 2s 0d	1797
200 perennials	£2 2s 0d	1799
48 Pinks	12s	1796
50 Pinks	12s 6d	1797
2 Indian Pinks in Pots – *Dianthus chinensis*	1s	1798
12 Pinks best	4s	1799

Plants ordered singly or in small quantities, alphabetically	Cost	Year
1 *Anagallis monilli* [sic] probably Anaglaais monellii	1s	1798
1 Strip'd Antirrhinum – hardy	1s 6d	1798
1 *Athanasia reflexa*	1s 6s	1798
1 *Athanasia flabulifera* [sic]	1s 6d	1798
1 *Buckneria nova* [sic]	2s	1799
1 Cape Jessamine: probably *Gardenia jasminoides*	1s 3d	1798
3 German Carnations	4s 6d	1799
1 *Celsia arctica*	1s	1798
2 *Celsia linearis*	2s 6d	1798
1 *Celsia urticifolia*	1s 6d	1799
1 *Chironia frutescens*	2s	1798
1 *Chrysanthemum indicum*	1s 6d	1798
5 *Cistus leudons* [sic]: probably *C. ladanifer*	4s	1799
Daizies [sic]	2s	1799
1 *Diosma uniflora*	3s 6d	1799
1 *Echium album*	1s 6d	1798
5 Heaths of Sorts @ 2s	10s	1800
2 double Heaths	3s	1800
1 *Erica arborea*	2s	1799

Plants ordered singly or in small quantities, alphabetically	Cost	Year
1 *Erica abietina*	2s 6d	1798
4 *Erica carnea*	3s	1796
2 *Erica carnea*	2s	1797
1 *Erica carnea*	9d	1798
2 *Erica carnea*	2s	1799
4 *Erica carnea*	3s	1800
1 *Erica cerinthoides*	5s	1798
1 *Erica formosa*	5s	1798
1 *Erica imbricata*	3s	1798
1 *Erica mammosa*	3s 6d	1799
1 Mediterranean Heath for the Terras [*sic*] back Row	1s	1795
2 *Erica mediterranea*	3s	1798
2 *Erica mediterranea*: syn. of *E. carnea*; see above	1s 6d	1799
1 *Erica multiflora* for the Terras [*sic*] back Row	6d	1795
3 *Erica multiflora*	2s	1796
4 *Erica multiflora*	3s	1797
1 *Erica multiflora*	9d	1798
2 *Erica multiflora*	2s	1799
4 multiflora [*sic*]: *Erica*?	3s	1800
1 *Erica multiflora alba*	1s	1797
3 *Erica multiflora alba*	3s	1800
1 *Erica persoluta*	2s	1798
1 *Erica persoluta*	3s	1799
1 *Erica planifolia*	2s 6d	1799
1 *Erica pubescens*	2s	1799
1 *Erica pulchella*	2s 6d	1798
1 *Erica pyramidalis*	5s	1798
1 *Erica simpliciflora*	3s	1799
1 *Erica taxifolia*	5s	1798

Plants ordered singly or in small quantities, alphabetically	Cost	Year
1 *Erica uniflora*	2s 6d	1799
1 green & purple Heath for the Terras [sic] back row	1s	1795
1 *Erica viridi purpurea*	1s	1796
1 *Erica vulgaris alba*	1s	1799
1 Bot. Bay Geranium	2s	1799
1 *Geranium incarnatum*	2s	1798
1 *Geranium* Goldstrip'd	1s 6d	1798
1 *Geranium lanceolatum*	1s 6d	1798
1 *Geranium tricolor*	3s 6d	1799
1 *Geranium tricolor*	3s 6d	1798
1 *Glycine bimaculatum*	1s 6d	1799
1 *Glycine coccinea*	1s 6d	1798
1 *Glycine rubicundi*	1s 6d	1798
1 *Gnaphalium crassifolium*	1s 6d	1799
1 *Hebenstretia dentata*	1s 6d	1798
1 *Hebenstretia dentata*	1s 6d	1799
6 red *Hepaticas*	1s 6d	1797
3 blue *Hepaticas*	1s 6d	1797
1 *Hydrangia* [sic] *mutabilis*: prob. syn. of *H. macrophylla*	1s 6d	1798
1 *Hypericum coris*	1s 6d	1798
1 *Lavendula stoechas*	1s	1798
1 *Lotus jacobeus*	1s 6d	1799
1 *Mahonia pinnata*	1s 6d	1798
1 *Metrosideris citrina*	2s	1798
1 *Miloluca* [sic] *coronaria*: probably *Melaleuca*	2s 6d	1798
1 *Mimulus aurantia*	1s 6d	1798
1 Double Nasturtium	1s	1798
1 *Oedora prolifera*	1s 6d	1798
1 *Passerina filiformis*	2s	1799

Plants ordered singly or in small quantities, alphabetically	Cost	Year
1 strip'd Perewinkle [sic] for the Border on the left Hand	3d	1795
1 *Polygala heistoria*	2s 6d	1798
1 *Primula farinosa*	1s	1799
1 *Psoralea betuminosa*	1s	1798
1 *Rhexia Virginica*	1s	1798
1 *Salvia coccinea*	1s 6d	1798
1 *Sedum*	1s	1797
4 *Sedum latifolium*	4s	1800
4 *Sedum longifolium*	4s	1800
1 *Sophora myosophillim*	1s 6d	1798
1 *Statice sinuata*	2s	1798
1 *Verbena triphylla*	1s 6d	1798

Bibliography

Adams, Henry, *The Botanist's Repository*, London, 1799

Aiton, William, *Hortus Kewensis or A catalogue of the plants cultivated in the Royal Botanic Garden at Kew*, vol.2, printed for George Nicol, Bookseller to his Majesty, London, 1789

Austen, Jane, *Mansfield Park*, 1814

Batey, Mavis, 'William Mason, English gardener', Garden History, February 1973

Batey, Mavis, 'Poet's Feeling and Painter's Eye: Mason's Flower Garden', *Flowers in the Landscape, Eighteenth Century Flower Gardens and Floriferous Shrubberies*, Buckinghamshire Gardens Trust, 2006

Batey, Mavis, *Jane Austen and the English Landscape*, Barn Elms Publishing, London, 1996

Commander, John, ed., *Gilbert White's Year*, Scholar Press, London, 1979

Campbell, Susan, *A History of Kitchen Gardening*, Frances Lincoln, London, 2005

Curtis, William, *The Botanical Magazine; or, Flower-Garden Displayed*, various volumes and dates from 1790, London

Duthie, Ruth, *Florists' Flowers and Societies*, Shire Publications, Aylesbury, 1988

Evelyn, John, *Acetaria: A Discourse of Sallets*, 1699

Foster, Paul, & Standing, David, *Landscape and Labour, Gilbert White's Garden 1751–1793*, Selborne Papers No.2, 2005

Harrison, S.G., Masefield, G.B., Nicholson B.E., Wallis, M., *The Oxford Book of Food Plants*, Oxford University Press, 1969

Harvey, John H., *Early Nurserymen*, Phillimore & Co. Ltd, London and Chichester, 1974

Harvey, John H., *Early Gardening Catalogues*, Phillimore & Co. Ltd, Chichester, 1972

Hurst, Jane, *Hartley Mauditt House*, Townsend Litho, 2015

Hussey, Christopher, 'Herriard Park, Hampshire', Country Life, 1 July, 1965

Jeffery, Sally, 'John James and George London at Herriard: Architectural Drawings in the Jervoise of Herriard Collection', *Architectural History*, Vol.28, SAHGB Publications, 1985

Laird, Mark, *The Flowering of the Landscape Garden, English Pleasure Grounds 1720–1800*, Philadelphia, University of Pennsylvania Press, 1999

Le Faye, Deirdre (ed.), *Jane Austen's Letters*, 4th edn, Oxford University Press, 2011

Loudon, J.C., *An Encyclopaedia of Gardening*, 8 vols, 1838

Loudon, J.C., *The Landscape Gardening and Landscape Architecture of the late Humphry Repton, Esq: Being his Entire Works on these Subjects*, London, 1840

Lloyd-Verney, Colonel, *The Hampshire Militia, 1757–1894*, Longman, Green Co., London, 1894

Mayer, Laura, *Humphry Repton*, Shire Books, 2014

Miller, Philip, *The Gardeners Dictionary*, 1754

Miller, Philip, The Gardeners Kalendar, 2nd edn, London, 1765

Nelson, E.C. & Oliver, E.G.H., *Cape heaths in European gardens: the early history of South African Erica species in cultivation, their deliberate hybridization and the orthographic bedlam*, 2004

Murray, Rt. Hon. Lady Charlotte, *The British Garden*, vols I & II, 3rd edn, London, 1808

Musgrave T., Gardner C., Musgrave W., *The Plant Hunters*, Cassell & Co., London, 1998

Philips, Charlotte & Shane, Nora (eds), *John Stuart 3rd Earl of Bute, 1713–92, Botanical and Horticultural Interests and Legacy*, Luton Hoo Estate, 2014

Pink, Nicola, 'Improving Herriard: George and Eliza Purefoy Jervoise's Public Image', unpublished dissertation submitted in partial fulfilment of the degree of Eighteenth Century Studies, Faculty of Humanities, University of Southampton, 2013

Sandford, R., *The Hillier Manual of Trees & Shrubs*, 8th edn, London, 2014

Taylor, M. & Hill, C., *Hardy Plants introduced to Britain by 1799*, Julians Press, Wimborne, post 1972

Watson, William, ed., *The Gardener's Assistant*, vols I, III, & V, Gresham Publishing Co., London, from 1925 on

White, Gilbert, *The Garden Kalendar 1751–1771*, Scholar Press, London, 1975

Worsley, Lucy, *Jane Austen at Home*, Hodder & Stoughton, London, 2018

Picture credits

Jervoise of Herriard Collection: Hampshire Record Office

Front cover: 44M69/F10/82/3

Fig. 1   44M69/F10/82/1

Fig. 4, Fig. 5   44M69/P165

Fig. 6   44M69/19/61

Fig. 10   44M69/E13/4/2/18

Fig. 11   44M69/F10/82/14

Fig. 12   44M69/E13/4/2/18

Fig. 13, Fig. 29   44M69/P1/76

Fig. 16   44M69/E13/4/2/6

Fig. 19   44M69/E13/4/2/7

Fig. 26   44M69/P1/72

Hampshire Record Office

Fig. 2   34/M62/3

Fig. 7   15M84/P4/3/81

Fig. 24   44M69/P1/132

Fig. 35   21M57/D60/1

All other images
in numerical order

Fig. 3   Photo courtesy of Dr Sally Jeffery

Fig. 8   NPG D5801 © National Portrait Gallery, London https://www.npg.org.uk/collections/ accessed 14 April 2019

Fig. 9   https://www.pinterest.co.uk/woburnabbey/humphry-repton/ accessed 6 May 2019

Fig. 14   Google Earth, accessed 24 April 2019 (imagery date 4/9/2017)

Fig. 15   https://collections.vam.ac.uk/item/O636049/print/ accessed 16 April 2019

Fig. 17   Susan Campbell, *A History of Kitchen Gardening* (2005), p.68

Fig. 18   Photo courtesy of Hindringham Hall, Norfolk

Fig. 20   Photos courtesy of Susan Campbell

Fig. 21   Susan Campbell, *A History of Kitchen Gardening* (2005), p. 118

Fig. 22, Fig. 23   Photos: Sally Miller, May 2018

Fig. 25   Google Earth, accessed 24 April 2019 (imagery date 4/9/2017); photo, Sally Miller, May 2018

Fig. 27   National Archives, Kew, Works 38/349. http://www.nationalarchives.gov.uk/education/resources/georgian-britain-age-modernity/flower-garden/ accessed 14 April 2019

Fig. 28   www.biodiversitylibrary.org accessed 14 April 2019

Fig. 30, Fig. 31, Fig. 32   http://botanicus.org accessed 20 September 2018. Courtesy of Missouri Botanical Garden

Fig. 33   www.forgottenbooks.com accessed 16 April 2019

Fig. 34   https://www.biodiversitylibrary.org/bibliography/51972 accessed 24 April 2019

Fig. 36   Private collection

About this book

2018 marked the bicentenary of the death of Humphry Repton. During the year there was a project to compile a national database of Repton sites and, in order to contribute to that, a small group of HGT research team members reviewed the two authenticated (and a few doubtful) sites in Hampshire associated with Repton. The first searches at the Hampshire Record Office quickly revealed that it holds a very large archive relating to Herriard Park and the Jervoise family, owners of the estate since the early 1600s. As with all research, the first scratchings developed into full-blown excavations and we realized there was quite a story to tell about Humphry Repton and his client George Purefoy Jervoise at Herriard in the 1790s. An early visit there at the invitation of the present owners, Mr & Mrs Jervoise, confirmed our view.

The first task was to list and transcribe the primary source material, namely all the Jervoise family archive documents for the years Repton was involved there. This was a team effort that lasted over the summer and autumn of 2018. Once you get your eye in, 18th-century script is quite easy to read but the spelling can be erratic and the frequent use of abbreviations and the habit of writing vertically in margins – all to save wasting expensive paper– sparked some head scratching. Transcription led on to analysis: what were the documents telling us about what was happening at Herriard in the 1790s? To flesh out our analysis, we were locating and studying secondary sources and widening our focus to fix Herriard in its historical context.

A point came when we agreed that having got so far in our understanding we really should publish. Topics for analysis had already been apportioned according to each author's particular interests: Dee on the small flowering and ornamental plants; Eleanor on the fruit growing; Sheila on the vegetable produce of the kitchen garden; Sally took trees and shrubs, and wrote the introductory chapters and the narrative around the construction of the Repton-designed kitchen garden. In January 2019 we received a grant from the Hampshire Archives Trust towards the cost of publication. Through the spring and early summer of 2019 we have worked very harmoniously with our editor Sue Gordon and our designer Steve Cluett. We think the result is a tribute to our hard work and expertise and their great skills.

We have learned a lot, have improved our research skills and have ferreted down numerous enticing and rewarding rabbit holes. We have enjoyed the experience and we hope you enjoy reading this book.

Sally Miller